MW01199046

Hardwood Flooring

How to Install and Maintain Hardwood Floors

HowExpert with Marc Hagan

Copyright HowExpert™
www.HowExpert.com

For more tips related to this topic, visit HowExpert.com/hardwoodflooring.

Recommended Resources

- HowExpert.com – Quick 'How To' Guides on All Topics from A to Z by Everyday Experts.
- HowExpert.com/free – Free HowExpert Email Newsletter.
- HowExpert.com/books – HowExpert Books
- HowExpert.com/courses – HowExpert Courses
- HowExpert.com/clothing – HowExpert Clothing
- HowExpert.com/membership – HowExpert Membership Site
- HowExpert.com/affiliates – HowExpert Affiliate Program
- HowExpert.com/writers – Write About Your #1 Passion/Knowledge/Expertise & Become a HowExpert Author.
- HowExpert.com/resources – Additional HowExpert Recommended Resources
- YouTube.com/HowExpert – Subscribe to HowExpert YouTube.
- Instagram.com/HowExpert – Follow HowExpert on Instagram.
- Facebook.com/HowExpert – Follow HowExpert on Facebook.

Publisher's Foreword

Dear HowExpert Reader,

HowExpert publishes quick 'how to' guides on all topics from A to Z by everyday experts.

At HowExpert, our mission is to discover, empower, and maximize everyday people's talents to ultimately make a positive impact in the world for all topics from A to Z...one everyday expert at a time!

All of our HowExpert guides are written by everyday people just like you and me, who have a passion, knowledge, and expertise for a specific topic.

We take great pride in selecting everyday experts who have a passion, real-life experience in a topic, and excellent writing skills to teach you about the topic you are also passionate about and eager to learn.

We hope you get a lot of value from our HowExpert guides, and it can make a positive impact on your life in some way. All of our readers, including you, help us continue living our mission of positively impacting the world for all spheres of influences from A to Z.

If you enjoyed one of our HowExpert guides, then please take a moment to send us your feedback from wherever you got this book.

Thank you, and we wish you all the best in all aspects of life.

Sincerely,

BJ Min
Founder & Publisher of HowExpert
HowExpert.com

PS...If you are also interested in becoming a HowExpert author, then please visit our website at HowExpert.com/writers. Thank you & again, all the best!

Table of Contents

Introduction

History of Hardwood Flooring

Hardwood floors have been in existence for thousands of years and were reserved for the extremely wealthy until around the 17th century. Once the wood industry gained access to the abundance of trees in North and South America, hardwood flooring became more common. Before the 17th century, hardwood floors were hand-hewn and smoothed out with actual sand until the sandpaper's invention in the 13th century. Once sawmills were invented in the late 16th century, the hardwood flooring industry started to resemble the one we see today.

Hardwood Flooring Today

Today hardwood floors come in a wide variety of colors, sizes, and species. Colors can range from the almost white of maple to the dark black of ebony. Planks can come in different thicknesses and widths, ranging from thin 1/20th of an inch to a 3-inch stair tread. The most common thickness is 3/4th of an inch. Typical plank widths range from a narrow 1 ½ inch to as wide as 12 inches, with 2 ¼th inches being the most common, but special boards have been made several feet wide. There are dozens of species and subspecies of hardwood flooring, the most common being oak, cherry, hickory, maple, and walnut. Hardwood floors also come in various installation options with the advent of manufactured planks and wood-like products such as laminate and vinyl planking.

Chapter 1: Knowing Your Subfloor

The subfloor is the floor underneath the floor you see; this is the base where a hardwood floor will be installed. In some older homes, pre-1950's, the subfloor is made of fir planks and has been refinished and is exposed. Subfloors come in two basic categories: wood or concrete. To know which kind of subfloor you have, you will have to tear up the pre-existing floor.

Tearing up the Existing Floor

The only way to get to your subfloor and prepare it for your new hardwood floor is to remove the existing floor covering it. Various floors cover your subfloor, including carpet, laminate, linoleum, sheet vinyl, tile, VCT, vinyl planks, or even an existing hardwood product.

Removal of Baseboards

Baseboards will need to be removed to install a new hardwood floor unless another type of trim will be used, such as base shoe or quarter round. Caulking can also be used to cover or fill the expansion gap (explained in chapter 4); this is not usually recommended but is common when installing linoleum or sheet vinyl products. When baseboards are caulked and painted, they will need to be cut at the top for easier removal. Use a sharp razor and utility knife to cut into the wall at the top of the baseboard. Cut into wall perpendicular to the baseboard, dragging knife along the top of the baseboard. Make sure you cut all the way through any caulking or paint. This is done so that while removing baseboards, the paint will not be pulled off the wall. If baseboards are not caulked at the top or paint has not been spread along baseboards and walls, they will not have to be cut at the top. This will be noticeable by a visible gap between the baseboard and wall.

Once top baseboards have been cut, or there is a visible gap between baseboard and wall, use a hammer and flat pry bar to remove baseboard from the wall. Slide the long end of the pry bar into the gap behind the base, or where the gap would be if caulking weren't there, and hit the short end of the pry bar with a hammer to force it behind the baseboard. Force the pry bar down at least half the height of the baseboard using the hammer, and then pull the pry board toward you, away from the wall. Move along the entire wall and repeat this process until all the baseboards in the desired area have been removed from the wall. If you will reuse the removed baseboard, make sure to number the back of the baseboard and the wall that it was removed from with the same number, so you know where it goes. Nails in the baseboards should be pulled through the back of the baseboards using nail pullers or pliers. Nails in the walls can either be removed using nail pullers or pliers, or they can be pounded over with a hammer. Pound nails over, not into the wall, because although it is rare, a pipe or wire might be behind the nail.

Tearing up Carpet

Carpet is by far the easiest and quickest type of floor to remove. Removing baseboards around the carpet's edges first will make the carpet a little easier to take up but is not necessary for carpet removal. Pull up the carpet from one of the corners, or an area that is already coming up, for easier removal. If the carpet is hard to get up by hand, cut into it with a utility knife or carpet knife, or pull from the corner using channel locks, pliers, or vise grips. After pulling the carpet away from all the tack strip underneath, cut it into manageable sizes, and roll it up into rolls as tight as possible. In many states, carpets can be recycled. Check on the Carpet America Recovery Effort (CARE) to see if your state is one of these states.

Underneath the carpet, there will be some foam padding. The foam padding will either be glued down or sometimes stapled if the subfloor is wooden. Either way, the easiest way to take up the foam pad is using a floor scraper, typically a 4-inch. Pull the foam pad up as you move the scrapper along with the glue or staples. Make sure to scrape up all glue or staples; both glue and staples are usually placed near the foam padding edges and seams. Once the foam padding is pulled away from the subfloor, you can roll it up and dispose of it. Really old padding might be really worn and start to fall apart. In such a case, the best way to remove it is with a broom and dustpan.

Along the edges of the carpet, there are strips of wood with tiny nails, or tacks, sticking up called tack strip.

Tack strip is nailed into the subfloor, whether it is wooden or concrete. A hammer and pry bar can be used to take up the tack strip in both cases, but a rotary hammer is much faster. With wooden subfloors, a pry bar can often be used alone because the nails are easier to get out of wood. When using a pry bar and hammer, place the pry bar with the corner of the long end pointing toward the nails in the tack strip and hit with the hammer until the nail releases from the subfloor. When using a rotary hammer, use a chisel bit and point one of the corners at the nails to remove them quickly. Be careful when handling tack strip as it is loaded with a lot of very sharp tacks. An easy and safe way to dispose of the tack strip is to save a piece of foam padding or carpet and roll it all up together.

Carpet in commercial settings, or carpet tiles, are glued to the subfloor and are much more difficult to remove. This can be done with a 4-inch flooring scraper or a larger size such as an 8-inch or even a 24-inch, but this is not recommended. The easiest way to take up commercial carpet is by using a floor stripper. Floor strippers can be rented from hardware stores or flooring stores, and some companies specialize in floor removal.

Tearing Up Floating Floors

Next to carpet, floating floors, or floors that are not fastened into the subfloor, are one of the easiest to remove. Floating floors can come in laminate, vinyl, and engineered hardwood. Removing baseboards and all trim such as quarter round, end caps, reducers, t-moldings, or toe kicks is highly recommended before taking up a floating floor. All of these can be removed with a hammer and pry bar.

Once baseboards and trim have been removed, pick an end to start on, and start pulling up the floor. Floating floors are clicked together so they can be removed by folding boards towards each other at the seam and pulling away. Some floating floors will be really locked in together and will require you to fold a plank or raise it with a pry bar and then hit it near the seam with a hammer to loosen it up. In some cases, an entire row of boards can be folded up and pulled out at the same time.

Some floating floors will have some muffling pad or moisture barrier underneath called underlayment. These are thin layers of foam, plastic, or other materials that are taped together. The underlayment is usually thin enough to where you can fold it up or roll it all up together after cutting along the taped seams.

Tearing Up Nailed Down Floors

Hardwood or manufactured wood floors on wooden subfloors are typically nailed or stapled down. Hardwood and manufactured wood flooring usually have a tongue and a groove, but this is not always the case. The tongue is a protruding piece of wood that fits into the recess, or groove, on the opposite side of wooden planks. If hardwood or manufactured wood floors do not have tongues and grooves, then they will be top, or face, nailed or screwed.

If the floor is top or face nailed, the nails should be removed first before prying up the floor. If a board is already up or there is an easy spot to fit a pry bar in, then you can start prying up the floor without taking out the nails. Removing the nails first, with a cat's paw or pulling pliers, will make it much easier to pull up the floor. For the top screwed floor, it is highly recommended to unscrew the screws before prying up the floor. Top screwed floors will usually have plugs that should be taken out first using something thin and sharp such as a utility knife.

Most hardwood and manufactured wood floors are tongue and groove, so they interlock. They will be fastened with either cleat nails, flooring staples, or, if the floor is incredibly old, hand nails. No matter what fastener is used, they will be fastened into the tongue or protruding side of the planks at a 45-degree angle. Planks around the edge of the floor will be top nailed, as most nail guns, staplers, and even an old-fashioned hammer will not be able to fit between these planks and the walls. Determining where the tongues of the planks are will make them easier to remove.

If there are no loose boards or an easy section of the floor to get a pry bar into, the floor can be cut into using a circular saw, or plunge-cutting saw. If using a circular saw, set the saw to the depth of the floor by checking near an exposed edge of the floor. There might not be any exposed edges, so you might have to look in a floor vent. I there are no exposed edges, a plunge-cutting saw would be more useful. Cut into a board until you feel the resistance from the saw change; this means you hit the subfloor. Hammer the pry bar into the newly made cut and pry up the board. Once you have pulled up a board, hammer the small end of the pry bar under the tongue side of planks and pull away from the plank. This will be the easiest direction to pull the planks out as this is how the nails or staples were originally put into the floor. A demolition bar can be used for even easier removal after finding the best way to get under the planks.

Tearing Up Glued Down Floors

One of the hardest types of floors to tear up are glued down floors. Raw hardwood is usually not glued down, but it can be. However, manufactured wood is almost always glued down to concrete subfloors. The amount of glue the previous installer used, the type of glue, and the amount of moisture in the subfloor all will affect how easy it will be to tear the floor up. If the previous installer used a smaller trowel when spreading the glue on the subfloor, there would not be much transferred to the floor, making it easier to take up. An inferior glue, or a glue that has been compromised in some way, such as partially drying before installation, will also make the floor easier to take up. All concrete subfloors have some moisture content; the higher the moisture content, the easier the floor will be to remove.

When deciding where to start taking up a glued down wood floor, if you cannot find loose boards or an exposed edge, knock on the floor to find a hollow spot. A hollow spot will sound different than the rest of the floor, almost like you are knocking on a door, and will indicate a spot where the floor has not completely bonded to the subfloor. If you have an area with a loose board or an exposed edge, use a hammer and pry bar or a rotary hammer to start prying up the floor. If you start from a hollow spot, use a chisel and hammer, or a rotary hammer with a sharp enough bit to chip out a hole in one of the boards. Once there is a hole, you can start to take up the floor with a hammer and pry bar, or the rotary hammer.

If the floor is glued down well and is hard to take up in full boards, use a circular saw to cut the floor into little square pieces. Find the depth of the floor and set the saw to that depth. Once the saw is set, cut the floor into 4-inch by 4-inch squares approximately. Run the saw along the length of the floor and along the width. Once the floor is cut up into little squares, use a rotary hammer to start taking up the square pieces. If the floor is still too difficult to take up, a turbo stripper or floor stripper can be used. There will usually be small pieces of wood and glue leftover that can be taken off using a floor scraper.

There are other types of glued down floors such as VCT (vinyl composition tile), linoleum, and vinyl sheeting. These products all use a very thin layer of glue that can be spread over concrete or wood subfloors. Like other glued down floors, the moisture content of the subfloor and the glue quality will determine how easy the floor will be to take up. VCT and other tile-like products can usually be taken up with some sort of flooring scraper, either a 4-inch one or larger. Linoleum and sheet vinyl products can often be taken up by hand or with a flooring scraper if they are stuck down well. If sheet products are particularly hard to remove, pouring some water over them can help when scraping them off.

Tearing Up Tile

Tile is sometimes one of the easiest types of floors to take up, and sometimes it is one of the most difficult. If the mortar or thinset used to fasten the tile is not very adhesive, or if the subfloor is wood or concrete with high moisture content, the tile will be easy to take up. Sometimes knocking on the tile will tell you if it is fastened well; it will have a hollow sound. If the tile is not fastened well, it can be taken up with a hammer and pry bar. If the tile is really not fastened well, it can be taken up with a pry bar alone. Usually, poorly fastened tiles will come up in full pieces.

If the tile is fastened to the subfloor well, it will come up in small pieces and take a lot of effort. If this is the case, a rotary hammer will be much more effective than a hammer and pry bar. When taking out tile, make sure to wear gloves and eye protection because it tends to fly around and can be very sharp. After taking up the tile, there will be pieces of the thinset leftover that can be removed using a flooring scraper.

Checking the Quality of the Subfloor

Once you have removed the existing floor, you will be able to assess the quality of the subfloor beneath. The subfloor should be checked for levelness, moisture content, soundness, and any possible defect that could affect the floor.

Wood Subfloors

The first thing to check for in wooden subfloors is any possible damage. If there are deep cracks, large holes, loose boards, or water damage, make sure to address these issues. Deep cracks should be filled with some wood filler or putty. If the crack is so large that it compromises the floor's structural integrity, replace the board. When holes in the subfloor are so large that they cannot be patched with a wood filler or putty, replace the board. If a board is loose, make sure to tighten the existing fasteners using either a drill or hammer and nail set, whichever is necessary. If there is any water damage in the subfloor, make sure to stop the water source and then repair the area.

 After checking for damage, the next thing to check for is levelness. The easiest way to check if the subfloor is level is to use a flooring straight edge. The longer the straight edge, the better. Of course, the straight edge should be able to fit in the area you are leveling. Straight edges range in lengths from 2 feet to 22 feet. Put the straight edge on the subfloor and move it around the area in different angles and spots. If a subfloor is unlevel, it will have dips, also called valleys, humps, also called peaks, or some combination of the two. If the subfloor has dips, these can be corrected using a self-leveling compound. Mix the self-leveling compound according to its directions and pour into the trouble areas. Drag the straight edge across the self-leveling in the dips to level them out. After the self-leveling dries, slide a flooring scraper across the top to smooth it out. If the subfloor has humps, they will need to be sanded down using some power sander. If the humps are so large that a significant amount of the wood would be sanded off, causing a loss of structural integrity, a self-leveling compound may need to be poured around the humps to raise the rest of the subfloor to the height of the humps.

Another possible defect of subfloors is unwanted creaks or cracking sounds. Creaks and cracks are usually caused by the subfloor's wood or the joists holding the subfloor rubbing against something. Sometimes, the subfloor is rubbing against the joists. Sometimes, it's rubbing against another board in the subfloor. Sometimes, the subfloor is rubbing against a nail. Once you pinpoint the noise's location by walking around the subfloor, tighten up the fasteners, whether nails or screws, in that area. If this does not stop the noise, it might be the joists themselves making the noise. If the joists cause the noise, you will have to remove the subfloor itself and tighten up the joists underneath.

Concrete Subfloors

The first thing to check in the concrete subfloor is any large cracks in the foundation. Cracking is normal in concrete subfloors, but if the cracks are so large that one side of the crack is raised higher than the other side, there may be problems with the soil the foundation is sitting on. If cracks are less than a quarter-inch wide, or a quarter-inch high, the area can be fixed by pouring a self-leveling compound. Cracks do not need to be filled if they are not raised up on one side. If cracks are severe, you might want to conduct a moisture test on the concrete slab to see if the moisture content is within tolerance. A moisture test will also need to be conducted if you will glue a floor down to the subfloor. If the moisture content is high, anything higher than 75% for glued down floors or 85% for non-glue downs, a company specializing in moisture removal will need to be called in to deal with the issue.

If cracks are not very severe and the moisture content is at an acceptable level, the next thing to check for is levelness. Once again, the best way to check a subfloor's levelness is to use the biggest flooring straight edge that will easily fit in the area. Slide the straight edge across the floor and move it around at different angles to look for dips and humps. Dips can be corrected by using a self-leveling compound in the affected area. Pour the leveling compound in the area and slide the straight edge across the area to level it out. Once the self-leveling is dry, smooth it out by sliding a flooring scraper across the top to take away bumps or raised edges. If there is a hump in the subfloor, it will need to be grinded down using either a concrete planer, cup grinder, or a floor grinder. Start by grinding the middle of the hump and move outwards until the hump is level with the rest of the floor.

Once your subfloor is free of all damage, level, and stable enough, you can move on to picking the product you want to install. There are several different wood and wood-like products that have their benefits and setbacks.

Chapter 2: Picking Your Product

Several different products can fit different needs, including cost, durability, flexibility, longevity, and installation ease. There are three major categories of wood floors: raw hardwood, manufactured wood, and wood-like products. Each of these products has differences that make them ideal for certain situations and impractical in others. The amount of time, money, and of course, one's personal preference are typically the determining factors in which product to choose.

Raw Wood

Raw wood includes both hardwoods and softer woods that are solid pieces of natural raw material. Raw woods come in various species that range in color, grain pattern, and hardness. The most common hardwood flooring is made from oak, cherry, hickory, maple, and walnut, with oak being the most common. Some older homes have fir subfloors that are refinished and used as a floor. There are, however, dozens of species and subspecies, including alder, white ash, bamboo, beech, birch, bubinga, American cherry, Brazilian cherry, cypress, ebony, hickory, kempas, Asian mahogany, Santos mahogany, maple, merbau, mesquite, red oak, white oak, padauk, pecan, pine, heart pine, sapele, Brazilian teak, true teak, tigerwood, American black walnut, Brazilian walnut, wenge, and even more exotic woods. They can also be milled into almost any width, length, and thickness.

The most common raw hardwood flooring is 2 ¼ inches wide by ¾ inch thick oak. If you already have a hardwood floor in your house, chances are this is the kind of floor you have. The benefits of this kind of floor include decent cost, durable, easy to acquire, easy to sand, and accepts stain and finish very well. Most wood suppliers and hardwood flooring stores will also have coordinating trim pieces such as baseboard, endcaps, reducers, t-moldings, stair treads, and toe kicks on hand. Other raw wood might not be in stock at wood suppliers or flooring stores and may have to be special ordered. Oak comes in two subspecies: red and white, and four grades: clear, select, number 1 common, and number 2 common. Red oak is a little easier to sand than white oak because it is softer. The grades determine the amount of color variation in grain pattern, knot holes, mineral streaks. Clear, as the name suggests, has the least amount of character flaws such as knot holes and mineral streaks and has the least amount of color variation. Number 2 common has the most variation and character flaws, but sometimes this is the preferred product if you want your floor to have a lot of character.

The species of wood you pick for your floor is usually based on color preference, but this doesn't have to be the case as there are a wide variety of stain colors that can be applied to the standard oak floor to make it appear as if it were another species. If one wants their floor to have a unique look, they can go with an exotic wood species other than oak. Some species are also a little more durable than oak floors, and some are a lot less durable. Some floors have special characteristics that might make them ideal for specific climates and environments. Bamboo is not a particularly durable floor, but it is somewhat moisture-resistant, so it is ideal for humid climates such as the Southeast or Hawaii. Maple is particularly hard, making it ideal for high use and high traffic areas such as gymnasiums or dance halls. However, maple is somewhat brittle, so it isn't easy to sand. Very dense woods may be durable, but that same density also makes it difficult for them to accept stain and finish. Some woods can be so exotic that it is challenging to find trim pieces to match the floor, so they will have to be special ordered, which can cost you a fortune in shipping fees. I have personally heard of a person spending thousands of dollars to have ebony shipped in from Africa.

The ultimate factor in determining which hardwood floor species to go with is your personal preference and the amount of money you are willing to spend on your floor. A specific species' color can often be imitated with special stains, but floors' grain patterns and characteristics may require special techniques. Knot holes and wormholes can be imitated using distressing techniques. All species can be milled into specific lengths and widths if you are willing to pay the price to have them specially milled. Remember, though, that the wider the plank of natural wood, the more likely the floor is to buckle, or "cup". Cupping is when the planks' edges start to rise off the subfloor, and you get a wave-like effect on your floor. This waviness of your floor can be sanded down, but the high spots will be sanded much more than the low spots in the floor, meaning these spots will wear away much faster. Thinner planks make it to where cupping isn't as much of a factor, but the thinner the planks are, the longer it takes to install them.

No matter what species of hardwood you get, they all have some common drawbacks. All hardwoods, even bamboo, are susceptible to moisture damage and will be affected by prolonged exposure to moisture. They also expand and contract with temperature changes, so they must have room for this expansion and contraction. Unless the planks are prefinished, they will also have to be sanded and finished after installing. Even if the flooring is a prefinished product, you will have to make sure the subfloor is completely level, or you may get edges sticking up. You can avoid all these drawbacks by choosing a manufactured wood product or a wood-like product such as laminate or vinyl planks.

Manufactured Wood

Manufactured wood flooring, or engineered hardwood, comes in various colors, patterns, sizes, and, maybe most importantly, installation options. Engineered hardwood is made from a top layer of hardwood with and under layers made from plywood. The layers are glued together with an adhesive and pressed together under high pressure, then heated to a high temperature. Unlike raw wood, engineered hardwood isn't as susceptible to moisture, usually comes prefinished, so it doesn't require the sanding and finishing process, and is readily available to purchase.

There are engineered hardwood products made to match the look of pretty much every species of natural raw wood out there. Engineered hardwood also comes in a variety of specialty finishes, such as distressed looks and unnatural colors. Sizes can range from a narrow 2 inches to a wide 12 inches. Without as much of a propensity to buckle or cup as raw wood, engineered hardwood is the way to go if you want wide plank flooring. Trim pieces and stair nosings will also be made to match engineered floors, not to have to be specially ordered as they would be for exotic species of raw wood.

One of the main draws of engineered hardwood flooring is that it has several different installation options. Raw hardwood flooring is limited to either nailing it down to the subfloor or gluing it down, although gluing it down is not the recommended installation method. Engineered hardwood can be nailed down, glued down, and installed as a floating floor if the product has a locking mechanism. Unlike raw hardwood, engineered hardwood is the recommended product to be used when gluing down your floor to a subfloor. Because it can be installed as a floating floor, meaning a floor not fastened to the subfloor, you can install a product without having to use a nail gun, nails, or expensive glue.

There are, of course, some shortcomings of engineered hardwoods that are similar to raw woods. Like raw wood, engineered hardwood will tend to expand and contract with temperature changes, however not as much as raw wood. Engineered hardwood can also buckle or cup but is nowhere near as susceptible as raw hardwood is. Because it is made partially from raw hardwood, there is a limited number of colors and grain patterns to choose from, but not as limited as choosing from raw hardwood itself. If in a high foot traffic area or area that gets used a lot, like raw hardwood, there may be a tendency for engineered hardwood to scratch. Like raw hardwood, engineered hardwood can be sanded and refinished if it has a large enough wear layer. The wear layer is the layer that can be sanded, the top layer of the product. The thicker the wear layer, the more times you can sand the product.

Engineered hardwood and raw hardwood are around the same price for the product, but the cost of installing engineered hardwood is usually a lot less. Due to its lower price, larger variety to choose from, and ease of installation, engineered hardwood is the better choice for the person trying to install their floor. Some products are cheaper and easier to install than both raw hardwood and engineered hardwood.

Wood-like products

There are products made to look like wood made with little wood or no wood at all. The two wood-like products that look the most like real wood are laminate and vinyl planks. Each has its advantages and disadvantages.

Laminate

Laminate flooring came into being in the late 1970s and has been a popular alternative to raw and engineered hardwood floors ever since. Laminate is made of multiple layers bound together with adhesives, pressed together, and heated to high temperatures. The top layer is the wear layer made of a clear hard substance that covers the next layer, which is an image usually made to look like some wood. The base of the laminate is made of particleboard, small pieces of wood glued together. Some laminate products will have a foam layer on the bottom, acting as a floor muffler to quiet the floor from possible debris underneath. Most laminate products do not have this feature, and an underlayment, product laid underneath the flooring, will need to be purchased.

Laminate flooring comes in various colors, patterns, and sizes that look remarkably similar to wood. Laminate can also come in colors and styles that look like distressed floors, stained woods, or not like wood at all but closer to stone or tile. Because there is a clear wear layer covering the image underneath, laminate is scratch-resistant, making it ideal for high traffic areas. The bottom layer of laminate is moisture resistant so that it can be laid over subfloors with high moisture content. There are also moisture barriers that can be used with laminate to make it better for high moisture areas. Laminate is one of the most economical types of floor covering you can buy compared to raw wood and engineered hardwood. One of the main draws of laminate, other than its durability and low price, is its ease of installation.

Laminate floors are floating floors, so they have a locking mechanism and can be installed without fastening them to the subfloor. This means they can be installed without the use of specialty tools, nails, or glue.

Although laminate is both moisture resistant and scratch resistant, there still can be problems. Excessive amounts of moisture, or continual exposure to moisture such as in a bathroom or kitchen, or from an animal urinating in the same spot, laminate will swell. It may be hard to scratch laminate, but once there is a scratch under the wear layer, there is no way to fix it as laminate cannot be sanded. Laminate is also very brittle, so it is prone, making it hard to work with when you are installing it. If you want a completely waterproof product, has a larger wear layer, is flexible, and you are not worried about spending a little more money, there is a better product for you.

Vinyl Plank Flooring

Vinyl plank flooring is like laminate in that it has a wear layer, image layer, and installed as a floating floor, but other than that, they are much different. Vinyl planks are not made of wood at all, but fiberglass, polyvinyl chloride (PVC), and of course, vinyl. Vinyl flooring has been around since the mid-1800s, but vinyl planks weren't invented until the 1970s. With innovations, vinyl flooring is quickly becoming the choice of professionals and do it yourself people everywhere.

Like laminate, vinyl planks come in a variety of colors, styles, and sizes. Vinyl planks can come in patterns that look like raw wood, distressed wood, tile, stone, and other material. Vinyl planks also come in sizes such as 12 inches wide by 24 inches long or 18 inches wide by 24 inches long, which look remarkably like tile. Most vinyl plank products also come with a foam or rubber pad on the bottom, eliminating the need for an underlayment. This will be one less cost to pay and one less step in the installation process.

Unlike raw wood, engineered hardwood, and laminate, vinyl plank flooring is completely waterproof, making it ideal for high moisture areas such as bathrooms, kitchens, and laundry rooms. If a liquid is spilled on the floor or some leak occurs, the floor can be dried out. Vinyl planks typically have a larger wear layer than laminate and are more resistant to scratching.

Vinyl planks are more flexible than laminate, so they are not as brittle and less prone to chipping. Because vinyl is more flexible, it is also easier to install and can be installed in areas that are not completely level. The fact that vinyl has no wood in it means it does not expand and contract like raw wood, engineered hardwood, and laminate. There is also no acclimation process for vinyl products. This means you do not have to leave the planks in the area where you will install them for some time before doing so.

Vinyl planks cost more than laminate, but there is usually no extra cost for underlayment as it is typically attached to the planks already. Vinyl also has several different installation methods, including glue down, peel and stick, and a floating floor. Due to its ease of use, durability, the fact that it is waterproof, and its multiple installation methods, vinyl is one of the top choices of professionals, do it yourself people, and homeowners looking for a great product.

After looking at the many different products, you can determine which one is best for your needs or most suits your preference. All products have their pros and cons, and all will add different values to your house or the project you are working on. Once you have your product picked out, you can now start to figure out how you will get it onto the subfloor.

Chapter 3: Preparing the Subfloor

Once you have picked a product to cover your subfloor with (details in the previous chapter) and leveled out your subfloor (details in chapter one), you can prepare your subfloor for installation. The subfloor's preparation will depend on what product you decided to go with and what kind of subfloor you have. Some products will require less preparation of the subfloor, and depending on the combination of product and subfloor, they may require quite a bit of preparation.

Wood Subfloors

Depending on the product, a wood subfloor could be somewhat difficult to prepare for installation. If you are installing a product that will be nailed down, it cannot be leveled out using a self-leveling agent like discussed in chapter one. If you will pour a self-leveling agent and the subfloor is a tongue and groove fir, it will also require additional preparation. The product will determine what you must do to the subfloor to prepare it for installation.

<u>Raw Wood</u>

Raw hardwood is recommended to be nailed down to a wooden subfloor. Nailing or stapling down to a wooden subfloor means you cannot pour self-leveling concrete to level the floor like you would in most situations. The self-leveling will level the floor out, but once you nail into the self-leveling agent, it will crack and crumble. Crumbled self-leveling under any floor will create a cracking or popping sound when you walk over the spot.

 The best way to level out a wooden subfloor with humps is to sand them down with some sander. If the humps are really high, and sanding will reduce the subfloor's structural integrity, the subfloor may have to be taken up and re-sheeted with plywood. If there are dips in the subfloor, they can be fixed by fastening thin pieces of plywood in the dip and sanding around the edges to smooth the area out. If the dips are shallow, they can be built up with a thick felt product. If the dips are not very deep and the humps aren't very high, the floor can be nailed to the subfloor without any leveling, but this will require extra sanding of the raw wood itself to level the floor out.

Before you do any nailing down of raw wood, you will have to lay down an underlayment. In the case of raw wood, the underlayment will have to be some moisture barrier. Some choices include rosin paper, tar paper, felt, and the most common option is a product called Aquabar "B." Rosin paper is not recommended by the National Wood Flooring Association (NWFA) but is commonly used in certain regions and amongst certain companies with that preference. If using rosin paper, tar paper, a thin felt, or Aquabar "B," roll the underlayment out and cut to size with a utility knife, then overlap all edges at least 4 inches. If using a thick felt, butt the edges of the felt together and tape the seams with heavy-duty tape. None of the underlayment options must be fastened to the subfloor as puncturing the barrier is not recommended. You can staple the underlayment down with a stapler that will not puncture all the way through the product. Once your underlayment is all in place, you are ready to start installing your product.

Engineered Hardwood

Because engineered hardwood has so many installation options, there are different ways to prepare the subfloor. If you are nailing or stapling the engineered hardwood to the subfloor, follow the previous instructions on preparing a wooden subfloor for raw wood. However, engineered hardwood can only be lightly sanded, so you must level out the subfloor to within an acceptable tolerance before installing the product.

Suppose you are going to glue down engineered hardwood to a wooden subfloor (something that I do not personally recommend). In that case, preparing the subfloor is easier than preparing for a nailed or stapled down floor. I do not recommend gluing down a floor to a wooden subfloor because if you ever plan on removing the floor, it can be extremely difficult and damage the subfloor. You can level out the floor the same way as mentioned in the previous section about raw wood, or you can pour a self-leveling compound and level out the floor, as mentioned in chapter one. Once the self-leveling compound has dried, you will have to scarify the floor using a buffer and a copper wheel. Scarifying is scraping the subfloor lightly so the glue will bond to the floor properly. After scarifying the floor, makes sure to vacuum it to remove all dust and debris. Once the floor is all leveled, scarified, and clean, it will be ready for installation of the product.

One of the easiest types of floors to prepare a subfloor for are floating floors. If you install an engineered hardwood product as a floating floor, see the next section on floating floors. If you are also pouring a self-leveling compound over a tongue and groove subfloor, see the next section.

Floating Floors

Floating floors require the least amount of preparation because they are not fastened to the subfloor and have a thick layer of underlayment that compensates for small imperfections in the subfloor. Subfloors can be prepared for floating floors by following all the previous instructions in the earlier sections of this chapter and chapter one.

One special case for leveling out a subfloor with a self-leveling compound is if you are laying over a tongue and groove subfloor. It is not recommended that you pour self-leveling over tongue and groove subfloors. The only time I would personally suggest doing this is if you do not want to spend a large amount of money on removing and replacing your entire subfloor. Remember this is not recommended but can be done if you absolutely must. The first step is to make sure the subfloor is fastened to the joists as tightly as possible. This can be done by setting all nails in the subfloor or tightening the screws. Additional nails or screws can be placed in the subfloor to tighten it up a little more. After tightening the subfloor up, vacuum to remove all debris, and then apply a multi-surface primer for self-leveling compounds. Make sure to get a primer compatible with the self-leveling compound and follow the directions on the container. After allowing the primer to set up, fasten a diamond mesh lath to the subfloor's deepest dips. The diamond mesh lath can be fastened using a staple gun, crown stapler, or hammer tacker. Staple from the middle of the mesh, moving your way out towards the edges, placing staples about 6 inches apart from each other. Make sure to staple the edges and hammer down any edges that stick up. Once you have applied the primer and diamond mesh, you can pour your self-leveling compound as you normally would. If the self-leveling starts to crack when dried, you can pour more and skim it over the top into the cracks. Repeat this process until cracking stops; this can be done whenever you have cracks in a dried self-leveling compound.

Once your subfloor is all leveled out, you can lay out your underlayment that goes with your product. If you have a moisture barrier and a floor muffler or underlayment, place the moisture barrier down first. Roll out the moisture barrier and cut to size with a utility knife, then overlap at least 4 inches around the edges. The floor muffler or underlayment should also be rolled out and cut to size with a utility knife. Butt the edges of the floor muffler or underlayment together and tape them together using a heavy-duty tape. There is no need to fasten the underlayment to the subfloor, but it can be done if it makes it easier to work with. Underlayment tends to try and roll back into the shape it originally was. This can also be avoided by placing something on the underlayment to weigh it down; I typically use some of the product. Once the underlayment is properly in place, you can start to install the product.

Concrete Subfloors

Concrete subfloors are usually a lot easier to level out than wooden subfloors, but they can take a lot more time and money to fix if there are significant problems. It is common for concrete subfloors to have cracks, dips, and humps. If cracks are ¼ inch or larger or raised up more than ¼ inch, the subfloor may be on a subpar foundation or have a significant amount of moisture. If your subfloor is in such a condition, a surveyor may need to be called out to assess the foundation. If your subfloor is not in too bad a shape, you can prepare it for the product you picked out.

Raw Wood

Raw wood cannot be put directly onto a concrete subfloor because it is not recommended to be glued down due to moisture issues, and it can't be installed as a floating floor.

Concrete subfloors are constantly releasing moisture, which does not make them compatible with laying raw wood directly over them. However, a concrete subfloor can be sheeted with ¾ inch plywood, or a product known as screeds or sleepers can be used. Either of these methods will cost more time and money to install, but if you are set on raw wood, these are your best options.

Sheeting a floor with ¾ inch plywood will require some moisture barrier and a way to fasten the plywood to the subfloor. Plywood can be either glued to the subfloor or fastened with nails, pins, or screws driven into concrete. When gluing down plywood, you will have to first apply some moisture barrier such as epoxy, mastic, or resin. For the best results, follow the glue manufacturer's directions and recommendations. After finding out the most compatible moisture barrier for the glue, you are going to use, follow the moisture barrier's directions. Once the moisture barrier is ready and in place, you can spread your glue in the designated area. Follow the glue manufacturer's instructions for which trowel size and how to spread the glue. For the best results, spread the glue in an area just big enough to put the sheet of plywood down. If you put spread glue along the entire area, you may not have any room to work, and glue can start to dry in spots that you do not get to right away.

Fastening the plywood using fasteners such as concrete nails or screws is usually cheaper, easier, and faster. When fastening plywood to a concrete subfloor, make sure to use fasteners long enough to go through the plywood and securely fasten it into the subfloor. Since the plywood is ¾ inch thick, you would want to use fasteners that are at least 1 inch long or longer. Anything longer than 2 inches is overkill and will make it more difficult than is necessary to fasten the plywood down. Once you have your fasteners, you will need some way to fasten them in, such as a hammer, drill, or some power or pneumatic fastener. Before fastening the plywood down, make sure to lay down some moisture barrier; usually, a 6-mil polyethylene film is used. Roll out the film in the desired area and overlap all edges at least 4 inches. Ensure that the film goes up the wall enough to be placed behind the baseboard, anywhere from 2 to 4 inches. After putting the polyethylene film in place, there is no need to fasten it down, and the plywood can be placed over the top. Place plywood in the desired area and make sure to leave an eighth of an inch gap between plywood sheets. Leave a quarter of an inch gap between the wall and plywood sheets. For best results, install the plywood diagonally to keep seams in the floor installed with landing on the seams in the plywood sheets.

One more way that a raw wood product can be installed on a concrete subfloor is by using what are known as screeds or sleepers. Screeds or sleepers are kiln-dried 2 x 3 or more often 2 x 4-inch boards that act as a nailing base for your floor, instead of using sheets of plywood. As I will be referring to them from here on out, screeds or sleepers are kiln-dried, meaning they are heated in an oven to remove moisture. They come in various lengths ranging from around 18 inches to 48 inches. Before fastening sleepers, make sure the concrete slab is clean and free of debris. If the subfloor is unlevel, make sure to level it out using a self-leveling compound described in chapter one. Sleepers are fastened to the concrete subfloor using asphalt mastic, which works as a moisture barrier and an adhesive. Follow the asphalt mastic directions that you have chosen for your project and spread out over the concrete slab. The first area sleepers should be put in is around the perimeter of the room or area you are working in. Sleepers should be put into the mastic with the broad flat face down and perpendicular to the direction of the floor you intend to place on top of it. Make sure to space boards 6 to 7 inches apart on center, meaning the center of one board is 6 to 7 inches away from the next board. The ends of the sleeper should be staggered and overlap about 4 inches. For additional support, the sleepers can be fastened to the concrete using masonry screws known as tap cons. Once the sleepers are in place, they should look something like joists in a wooden subfloor, just staggered and in various lengths. After installing the sleepers, a layer of 6 mil polyethylene film should be laid over the top, overlapping at least 4 inches at the ends and running up the wall 2 to 4 inches.

Engineered Hardwood

Because engineered hardwood can be installed in so many ways, there are different preparation methods for the type of installation you will be using. If you are going to install the engineered hardwood by nailing it down, you can follow one of the previous section's methods on raw wood. Engineered hardwood is typically installed; however, it would be easiest and consistent with the subfloor.

On concrete subfloors, engineered hardwood is usually glued down and is one of the most common ways I have personally seen engineered hardwood floors laid over concrete subfloors. When preparing a concrete subfloor for a glue-down installation, the first thing to do is to inspect the floor for any major damage such as cracks wider or raised up more than a quarter inch. If there are issues such as these, the foundation of the house may need to be inspected. The second step in preparing a glue down floor is to conduct a concrete slab's moisture test. To conduct a moisture test, you will have to drill into the concrete slab about a third of the way. Most concrete slabs are 4 inches thick, so you will have to drill slightly deeper than an inch and 5/8 into the slab. For the best results, follow the directions of the moisture meter or RH tester you are using. Make sure to take readings in all the areas you will be installing the floor in; if an area is particularly large, more than 200 square feet, take readings in more than one area. Take readings 24 hours apart and over three days for the most accurate readings. If the slab is in good condition and within acceptable moisture levels, it can be leveled out. Once the subfloor is leveled out following the directions in chapter one, it can be scarified. Scarify the subfloor by running a buffer with a copper wheel with little spikes along the entire area where you will be gluing down the floor. After scarifying the floor, vacuum the area, and you will be ready to spread your glue.

If you install an engineered hardwood product as a floating floor, follow the directions in the next section on how to prepare your subfloor.

Floating Floors

Floating floors are one of the easiest products to prepare a subfloor for installation because they are not fastened down. Most floating floors are moisture-resistant, typically have a moisture barrier, or are completely waterproof, so you do not have to worry about the slab's moisture content. The only time to consider possible moisture problems are if you can visibly see them. Visible moisture problems are pools of water, mold, and possible foundational problems that would result in significant cracks, as discussed before. If there are no such problems, you can start with your standard floor preparation for floating floors.

The first thing to do when preparing a subfloor is to check for levelness and level it out with a self-leveling compound or grinder, as described in chapter one. After the floor is leveled out, scrape any high spots or uneven edges with a 4-inch flooring scraper. Once all the high spots and uneven edges are scraped down, vacuum up any dust and debris. If the product you chose already has some floor muffler or foam padding attached to it, you are ready to install it.

If the product you chose does not have an attached underlayment, you will have to place a corresponding underlayment in the designated areas. If you use some moisture barrier, usually recommended in wet areas such as bathrooms, kitchens, and laundry rooms, roll this out first. Roll out the moisture barrier in the designated areas, overlapping the ends at least 4 inches and rolling up the wall 2 to 4 inches. After your moisture barrier is in place, roll out your underlayment or foam muffler in the designated areas. All edges should be butted together about ¼ inch apart and then taped together with packaging or duct tape. If the underlayment has a stick together system on the side, you can use that, but you will still have to tape the ends on the short side of the roll. You will want to use something to weigh the underlayment down as you work with it because it tends to roll up on itself. I typically use the material itself. You do want to overlap the underlayment or foam muffler, and it does not need to be rolled up the wall at all. Once your underlayment is in place, you can give it one more vacuuming to remove debris, and you are ready for installation.

Glue Down or Peel and Stick Vinyl

The preparation for glue down and peel and stick vinyl is pretty much like glued-down engineered hardwood. The only difference in the products is that you will use different glue for glued down vinyl. The glue for glued down vinyl will be spread in a thin layer across the subfloor and will have to be left partially dry, a process called flashing. Once the glue has flashed, the product will be ready to install. Both wooden subfloors and concrete subfloors will have a similar preparation process; they should pretty much be flat and dry. Once your glue has flashed, follow the manufacturer's directions, the product will be ready to install. For peel and stick vinyl, once the floor is flat and dry, you will be able to install the product as the adhesive is already on the product.

One last step in floor preparation is undercutting. Undercutting is the process of cutting anything in the area you are installing your product in that you want to make it look like the floor is going underneath. This can include door casings, door jams, fireplaces, thresholds, cabinets or drawers that protrude out of the wall, and dividers in closets or kitchens. You will need to use a casing saw for all these instances, sometimes called a jam saw, or an oscillating multi-tool with the corresponding blade, such as a wood cutting or rock cutting blade for fireplaces. Blades on a casing or jam saw should be set to the thickness or height of the material you are installing. If you are using an underlayment with your product, make sure to get the height with the material and the underlayment. Once you have the correct height, you can undercut the areas that you want. If using an oscillating multi-tool, use a piece of the material and underlayment, if applicable, as a base to put your saw on and cut the desired area. If you decided not to undercut areas such as door casings and dividers, you would most likely have to use some caulking or silicone to fill the gaps between these areas. Trim pieces such as quarter round or baseboard can often be used around cabinets and fireplaces, but this will not work around door casings.

Always follow the manufacturer's directions and specifications on all products to make sure the subfloor is properly prepared for your designated product. Proper preparation of the subfloor makes the installation go as smoothly as possible. Taking care of all the major problems first will make sure that setbacks during installation and after are kept to a minimum. Now that your subfloor has been properly

prepared for the product you decided to go with, we
can move on to the bulk of the work, the installation.

Chapter 4: Installation

Finally, we have gotten to the point you have been waiting for, putting the actual floor in. Once all your preparation is complete, your new floor can finally become a reality. The product and the type of subfloor will determine the tools method you need to use for installation.

Raw Wood

Raw wood is recommended only to be nailed down to another type of wood because concrete has a certain moisture content. Moisture and raw wood do not work together well, so raw wood must be nailed down to a wooden subfloor, plywood over concrete, or a sleeper system. Whether nailing to a wooden subfloor, plywood over concrete, or a sleeper system, a flooring cleat nailer or flooring stapler will be needed for the major part of the floor; the size of the nails or staples will be determined by the thickness of the product and the subfloor. A 16-gauge brad nailer will be needed for the edges of the floor near walls and hard to reach areas; the nails' length will be determined by the thickness of the product and the subfloor. Hand tools needed will include a measuring tape, pencil, chalk line, hammer, tapping block, pry bar, and a flooring pull bar. Saws needed will include a miter saw, table saw, and a jigsaw if there are areas where boards need to be cut in a curve of some sort. Make sure your miter saw is large enough to cut the width of the planks you have. Once you have the correct tools, you can start to install your product.

Nailed to Wooden Subfloor

When nailing your raw wood product to a wooden subfloor, the product's thickness is what needs to be considered. If you are installing a half-inch thick product, cleat nails or staples and brad nails should be 1 ½ inch long and follow the manufacturer's recommendation for gauge size. Typically, a 16- gauge cleat nail is used for a stronger hold, and an 18-gauge is used to avoid splitting the tongue of the plank. Remember, when it comes to gauging size, the larger the number, the smaller the gauge. An 18-gauge staple is usually used for a half-inch thick product. For a standard ¾ inch thick product, use 2 inches long cleat nails or staples and brad nails. Once again, the cleat nails' gauge size will be determined by the manufacturer's specifications or whether you want more holding power or less tongue splitting. Staples should be 15 gauge. If installing a raw wood product that is thinner than ½ inch, see the section on nailed down engineered hardwood.

Once you have the right fasteners, you can determine the direction you want to go with your floor and start installing. A floor is typically installed with the room's length, meaning the floor is laid with the long side of the planks following the direction of where the room is longest. The direction is, however, is completely up to personal preference when laying on a wood subfloor. One thing to consider is the direction of the seams in the subfloor. You do not want the seams in the floor to land on one in the subfloor as it might somewhat reduce structural integrity.

Getting the Straight-Line Down

When you have a direction picked out, and your subfloor is completely prepared, you can start to mark out the area where your initial straight line will go. A straight line, as it sounds, is a straight line where you will begin your installation. The way you determine where your straight line will go is by measuring 12 inches off of a wall or some other object such as a carpet line or cabinet that will be running parallel to the direction in which you intend to lay the floor. Repeat this on the opposite side of the area as well. Walls, cabinets, and other objects are rarely ever perfectly straight, so the measurements are just used to get an idea of where the floor would look the straightest. Mark 12 inches away from the wall on one end of the room, and then mark 12 inches away from the same wall on the other end of the room. To check how straight the wall is or is not, measure from the opposite wall or object and see if the marks are the same distance from one another. Usually, the marks will be somewhat off; if you are lucky, they will be equidistant from both walls or objects, but this still does not mean the walls or objects you measure out are straight. There may be some sort of bow in the middle of the walls, making them off near the center. Either way, there are ways to compensate for a wall or walls being a little off in some areas.

You may have to split the difference between how much one mark is different than the other. This means that if your first mark is a quarter-inch further away from the opposite wall as your second mark, you will put a new mark next to your first mark a 1/8 of an inch closer to the opposite wall. This may be somewhat difficult to understand, but you are pretty much lining the straight line up with two opposite walls, both of which may not be straight, so you are looking for where the floor would seem to look the straightest. By the way, if your walls are only ¼ of an inch off, you are lucky; sometimes, you must try and compensate for over a 3 or 4-inch difference in walls. If you can't compensate for a difference in the walls by splitting the difference in a straight line, let's say because the walls are just so bowed, it's just not going to happen. There is a spacing technique that can account for some of this. Of course, you may have to deal with boards being wider at one end of the floor, both ends, or possibly even the middle of the floor. Once you have found where would be the best possible place to put your straight line, hammer a nail into the subfloor about ¼ to ½ of an inch in one of the marks you made, with enough of the nail sticking out to tie you chalk line to it. Go to the other end of the area where you put your other mark and line the chalk line up with it pulling tightly with one hand. Pull the chalk line up with your other hand and let go to snap it to the subfloor. If the line is not dark enough to see, you will want to repeat the process, possibly with a darker color chalk. If you are installing a standard 2 ¼ product, measure the width of 5 or 6 planks together, including the tongue. If the planks you are installing are wider products, use 2 to 4 planks, and measure the width. Use this measurement to make two new marks next to your first 2 marks and move into the room's center. Once again, snap a chalk line but now with these 2 new marks. You should now have two parallel chalk lines, one about 12 inches from the initial wall you measured from and one about a foot away from that.

Installation

Once you have the area for your straight line marked out, you can start to install your product into the straight-line area. Start by placing the grove side of a plank on the line closest to the wall and making sure it is lined up on both ends. Start from the middle of the area you are working in. Use your 16-gauge brad nailer to nail into the tongue side of the plank at a 45° angle, starting from one side of the plank and moving towards the other end. Nails should be shooting into the plank, not away from it. Place nails about 4 inches away from each other. Once you have the first plank down, you can place another plank at either of the small ends, known as butt-joints, and repeat the process. Make sure the butt-joints are fit tightly together using your tapping block. If the butt-joint will not close and you see a gap, you may need to use a hammer with your tapping block. Repeat this process all the way down the straight line until you get to the end of the area you are working in. Use your miter saw to cut the planks at the end to the right size, make sure to leave a ¼ inch gap at the ends to allow room for expansion of the wood. A quick way to get the size without using a tape measure is to turn the planks you are using for the end cuts the opposite way the floor is going. The tongue will be facing the opposite way. Push the end of the plank to the wall and put a mark on it where the previous plank ends. Remember to cut an extra ¼ inch off for expansion; now, you should have the proper length and correct end to butt to the previous plank. Repeat this on the opposite end of the area you are working in.

After your first row of planks is secure, you can place another plank in front of it, starting from one end of the row, and repeat the process. Make sure the tongues of the first row and the groove of the next row are securely fit together using a tapping block. If a plank does not fit into the planks of the first row just by lightly hitting it with the tapping block, you may have to use a hammer with the tapping block. It is common for planks to be slightly warped; if this is the case, you may have to step on the plank where it is warped while using the hammer and tapping block. Make sure that the butt-joints are more than 4 inches apart if you are using a 2¼ inch product, or at least the width of the planks if you are using a product that is wider than 4 inches. Finish 3 or 4 rows in this same fashion, and then you can start to use your flooring stapler or cleat nailer. When using either a flooring stapler or cleat nailer, make sure to change the spacing plates to fit the size of flooring you are using. These plates will come with the stapler or nailer, and manufacturer instructions should be followed as to how to put them on correctly. Place staples or nails about 6 to 8 inches apart from each other. A hammer or rubber mallet will be needed to operate the flooring stapler or cleat nailer; see manufacturer's directions for details. Continue filling in the desired area with planks until you get to the end wall or end of the area you are working in. If there is a wall at the other end of the area you are working in, you will not be able to use your flooring stapler or cleat nailer about a foot away from the wall and will have to switch back to your brad nailer. The last few rows of the floor will have to be top nailed, meaning you will have to nail directly into the top of the planks. Nail directly in the center of the plank about 8 inches apart from each other. If the planks are larger than 4 inches, put two nails into the plank equally spaced from each other, and the plank's edges do the same thing about 8 inches away along the entire plank.

 Once you get close to a wall, you may have to cut a plank along the long side, known as ripping down a board. You can rip a board down to the proper width by measuring along the wall with a tape measure. Because walls are seldomly perfectly straight, the plank may be wider at one end. It will be easier to figure out how to make your cutting line by using another plank for measuring. Do this by putting the plank you want to rip down on top of the previous row and lining it up with that row. Next, use another plank and put it on top of the plank you want to cut while pushing it all the way against the wall with the tongue side touching the wall. Take a pencil and mark the plank on the groove side; this will give you your cutting line. Rip the plank down using a table saw. Place the ripped down plank in the desired spot and use a pry bar to pull it against the previous row while top nailing it in with your brad nailer. Repeat this process along the entire last row. You will also have to repeat this process on the opposite side of the area you are working in, the spot where you put the initial straight line. Because the row you started on has the groove side exposed, you will have to use a thin oval piece of wood, known as spline, to make a tongue on the groove side of this row. Place the spline into the groove and hit it all the way in using a hammer or tapping block. The spline can be purchased at flooring stores and some hardware stores. You will need enough to complete the entire row, but there can be gaps in between if both ends of the planks have enough spline to grab onto. Once the spline is in place, you can finish this side of the floor just like you did on the other side.

If you are installing in areas that have cabinets or counters that make it impossible to get some nailer into, you can glue the planks under this area using a strong adhesive. You will have to cut the moisture barrier out from underneath these areas so the planks can adhere to the subfloor properly. After the entire area is filled in with planks, with ¼ inch gaps around all edges, you will be ready for the sanding and finishing process discussed in the next chapter.

Nailed to ¾ Inch Plywood Over Concrete

If you are installing your product onto a subfloor built up with ¾ inch plywood over concrete, you will follow the instructions described above. The only difference in the installation is the size of the fastener you use. Brad nails and staples or cleat nails should be no longer than 1 ¾ inch if you install the standard ¾ inch thick raw wood. If the product you are using is thinner, the staples or nails should be the product's size plus one inch. This is done to ensure that the nails or staples do not go all the way through the plywood and puncture the concrete. You might ask how will a nail or staple that is the size of the product plus one inch not go through ¾ inch plywood? Remember that you are nailing at a 45° angle. When top nailing, use a brad nail that is ¾ inch plus the size of the product because these will not be shot in at an angle. Since the installation of raw wood is similar on ¾ inch plywood, you can follow the previous section's directions on nailing raw wood to a wood subfloor. After the installation is complete, you can move on to the next chapter about sanding and finishing.

Nailed to Sleepers

If you are installing your product over a sleeper system, you would once again follow most of the instructions above, with some exceptions. Because a sleeper system is not a complete or fully filled subfloor like a standard wooden subfloor or ¾ inch plywood over concrete, there are gaps that you will not be able to nail into. You will also not pick your direction; the floor will have to go in the opposite direction that the sleepers are going. If your product is less than ¾ inch thick, it is not recommended for installation over sleepers. Your product will have to be nailed into the sleepers using 2-inch brad nails and cleat nails or staples. Because there is some moisture barrier laid over the top of the sleepers, you will have to feel where the sleepers are and mark the area.

Once the sleepers are marked out, you can get your straight line down. Because you cannot just mark anywhere on the floor, you have to make your marks on top of the moisture barrier where the sleepers are located. It might be hard to snap a line if the moisture barrier is loosely fit to the sleepers, so you can staple the moisture barrier tightly to the sleepers to help with this. Once you have your two marks marked out as described in the previous section on getting the straight-line down, you can snap your straight-line. Once you have the straight-line area marked out, you can install your straight-line just as described before, except you must nail or staple the planks into the sleepers. Continue the rest of the installation just as described before by nailing or stapling into sleepers instead of every 6 to 8 inches. After completing the installation in the entire area, you can go to the next chapter on sanding and finishing.

Engineered Hardwood

Engineered hardwood has a similar look to that of raw wood without some of the drawbacks. Because it is prefinished, there is no need to sand and finish engineered hardwood, eliminating one step in the process to completion. Engineered hardwood also has less issues with moisture and more installation options, meaning it can be installed in a variety of areas. The installation method you decide to go with is usually decided by what kind of subfloor you are laying over. If you are laying your product over a wooden subfloor, the usual method is nailing or stapling it down. If you are laying over a concrete subfloor, the usual method is gluing it down. If you happened to get a product with a locking mechanism that can be installed as a floating floor, you could lay it over either a concrete or wood subfloor. Engineered hardwood is not recommended to be laid over a sleeper system as it is typically less than ¾ inch thick.

Nailed Down

When nailing or stapling down engineered hardwood to a wooden subfloor or plywood, use 18-gauge brad nails and 18-gauge cleat nails or staples. If your product is less than 5/16 of an inch, use 1 to 1¼ inch brad nails and cleat nails or staples. If your product is 3/8 to ½ inch thick, use 1¼ to 1½ inch brad nails and cleat nails or staples. If you have a product that is 5/8 of an inch thick, use 1½ inch brad nails and cleat nails or staples. For the initial straight-line and installation process, you would follow all the directions described in the section on nailing down a raw wood product described before. One difference between installing the engineered hardwood and the raw wood is that nail holes left from top nailing will have to be puttied on engineered hardwood floors. This is done by using a little piece of a painter's putty that matches the floor and rubbing it into the holes. After filling the holes, use a rag with a little bit of paint thinner to wipe any excess off. If something happens to the floor, such as deep scratching or gouging, the floor can be lightly sanded and refinished if necessary. If you have a distressed product or a product with a very thin wear layer, sanding is not recommended. However, the product may be buffed with a buffer, but this will only remove very minor scratches. If you are going to sand and refinish an engineered hardwood product, see the next chapter on sanding and finishing. If you are not going to sand and finish the floor, move to Chapter 6, "Trim."

Glued Down

Engineered hardwood is most often glued down when it is over a concrete subfloor. It can be glued down to a wooden subfloor, but this is not recommended if you ever intend to remove the floor in the future. Once an engineered hardwood product is glued down, it is extremely difficult to take up and often leave the subfloor damaged. For this section, we will assume the product will be glued down to a concrete subfloor. You will need a pencil, rubber mallet, masking tape, tapping block, pry bar, pull bar, a miter saw, and table saw for installation. If you are going to be making rounded cuts, you will need a jigsaw.

Just like when nailing down a product, the first thing that must be done for a glued down product is to get the straight-line down. Once again, you will need a tape measure, chalk line, pencil, hammer, and a nail that will drive into the concrete. Once you know what direction you want the floor to go, measure the distance from one wall or end of the area to the other end of the area. Measure the distance perpendicular to the direction of the floor. Measure one side of the room or area and then measure the other side of the room. Once you have the distance on both ends of the room or area, try to find the approximate center of the room or area. Just like discussed before, the walls may not be straight, so one side of the room may be a little wider than the other. Do your best to split the difference and mark the center on both sides of the room. Drive a nail into one of the marks and tie your chalk line around the nail. Pull the chalk line tight with one hand and line it up with the mark on the opposite side of the room. Once you have the chalk line lined up and pulled tight with one hand, use your other hand to pull the chalk line off the subfloor to snap the first line.

After snapping the first line:

1. Measure the width of 4 or 5 planks fit tightly together. If the planks are narrow, 3 to 6 inches, measure 5 planks.
2. If the planks are wider than 6 inches, measure the width of 4 planks.
3. Once you have the measurement, measure that same distance away from the first mark you made and make another mark.
4. Do the same thing at the opposite end of the room or area and make another mark that same distance away from your second original mark. The two new marks should both be on the same side of the old line; however, they can be made on either the left or right side of the first line.

Once you have your two new marks on the same side of the original line, you can hammer a nail into one of them and snap another chalk line just like before. You should now have two lines that are the width of 4 or 5 boards apart, spanning from one end of the room or area to the other.

Once your straight-line is marked out, you can start to fill it in with glue. Use a floor glue that is compatible with your product, and make sure to use a trowel that is recommended by the manufacturer of the glue. Some glue will have a trowel edge that can be attached to a flat trowel already in the bucket of glue. There is usually a top layer of dried glue on the top of the glue; make sure to remove this before starting. If there is a piece of plastic at the top of the glue, retain this for later; you may need to use it to keep the glue fresh. Pour glue in the center of your straight-line area and spread it around with the manufacturer recommended trowel. Trowel the glue starting from one side of the straight line, moving down and toward the straight line's center in a half-circle type motion. Do the same thing on the other side of the straight line, moving down and toward the center in a half-circle type motion. Hold the trowel perpendicular to the subfloor to ensure the correct amount of glue is transferred. The result should be a bunch of fan or semicircle shapes with grooves in them. For the best results, make sure to read all the manufacturer's directions. Fill in the area between the two lines of your straight-line completely. If the area you are working in is very long, only spread the glue about 15 to 20 feet along the straight line so one end doesn't start to partially dry or flashover before you can get to it.

Once the glue is down, you can start to fill in the straight line with planks. Line the groove side of one of your planks with one side of the straight-line; whichever side you choose is up to you. I like to face the planks' tongue side in the direction with the most obstacles, such as objects to lay around or weird angles. If the product you picked has varied lengths, as they typically do, start with the longest plank size first. If the planks are all the same length, just put a full plank down. After your first plank is down, place a shorter one in front of it facing the same direction and make sure to fit the second plank tightly together with the first using a rubber mallet. Be sure that there is a ¼ inch gap left between the wall and the ends of the 2 planks. The first plank may have moved when you were hitting the other plank with the mallet to fit them tightly together. If this is the case, make sure to line the first plank up with the straight line again. Once you have the second plank in place, you can put another plank at the end of this plank and in front of the first plank. Once again, make sure to fit the planks tightly together on all ends. Also, make sure to keep the butt joints, the area where the short ends of the planks meet, at least the planks' width apart, so if the planks are 4 inches wide, the butt joints should be at least 4 inches apart. If it is difficult to get the butt joints to close or get the planks to fit together, use a hammer and tapping block. After you put the third plank down, you can put a plank in front of it and the second plank, starting the third row. Once again, use a rubber mallet to fit this plank tightly to the second row of planks. Makes sure to stagger the sizes you are using, avoiding any pattern as this will ensure the floor's structural integrity.

If you have a plank that is smaller than the plank you put done in the third row, go ahead and put this one down starting the fourth row. Make sure you fit it tightly to the previous row with a rubber mallet and maintain your ¼ inch gap from the wall. If you only measured the distance of 4 planks for the straight-line, it should be filled in on this end. If it is filled in, take your masking tape and tape the rows together so they will not move. If you measured for 5 rows put another plank in the first row and fit all the joints tightly together. Place a new plank in every row after moving down until you have a plank in the fifth row ¼ inch from the wall. Now you can tape all the rows together with a strip of tape. Continue this process the entire way down the straight-line, making sure all planks are tightly fit together and that they are lined up on the straight-line. Once you get to the end of the straight-line, cut the planks at the end, making sure to leave a ¼ gap between the end cut and the wall. Make sure to tape the planks together by putting a strip of tape along the floor perpendicular to the direction of the floor; tape about every 3 or 4 feet. If you notice some butt joints moving apart, you can hit them together with the rubber mallet and tape them to stay in place. Put planks in the areas where the butt joints are, making sure that they bridge over the butt joint. Do this on both sides of the straight line and make sure the planks are fit tightly to the straight line's planks. These planks should not have glue under them and do not need to be in a full row with the butt joints all closed together. These planks are just used to help the initial straight-line setup. Once you have your straight-line filled in with planks, lined up properly, secured with planks bridging the exposed butt-joints, and taped together, you can let it sit for a day to dry or set up. You want to let the floor set up for a day so it does not move while you do the rest of the installation. Some installers will put weight on the straight-line, such as several boxes of the material, in order to continue with installation without waiting for the straight-line to set up. You can also lay the floor all the way to the wall and put wedges in between the wall and floor, but both methods still leave the possibility of the floor moving off-center. Make sure to put a piece of plastic in the bucket of glue before you put the cap back on to keep it from drying out too much if you will reuse it.

If the floor is going to be continuous throughout several rooms or areas, the initial straight-line will work for the entire continuous area. If you are gluing down your product in several different rooms or areas that are separated by some other floor, you will have to put a straight line down in every separated area. After you wait a day for your straight-line to set up, you can continue with the rest of the installation. Remove the planks you used to bridge the butt joints on the sides of the straight-line. Now that you know the distance of 4 or 5 planks from the initial straight-line, you can use this measurement for the rest of the installation. Make two new marks the distance of 4 or 5 planks, one on one end of the room or area and another on the other end, using the straight-line as your starting point to measure from. Both marks should be on the same side of the straight-line. It does not matter which side of the straight-line you work on as long as the marks are on the same side.

Once you have these two new marks, you can snap a new line as described before. Use this new line and the edge of the existing straight-line as the markers for where you will spread your glue. Spread the glue on the floor as described before. Make sure to get the glue as close to the straight-line without getting it in the grooves or on the tongues of planks. If you get some glue on the grooves or tongues, clean as much off as possible because if you do not, it will be hard to get the planks to fit together tightly. Once you have spread the glue using the correct trowel, you can install your product as described before. Remember to keep the butt joints the width of the floor apart from each other. Tape the floor as you go along, making sure to tape from the last row and overlap into the end of the initial straight line. Always keep a ¼ gap on both ends of the floor.

Once this area is complete, you can repeat the process:

- Snap another line.
- Fill it in with planks.
- Keep butt joints at least the width of the planks apart.
- Tape the floor tightly together, overlapping at least one row into the previous section.
- Maintain a ¼ gap on the ends.

When you are close enough to the wall or the edge of the area you are working in, you will no longer have to snap a line; fill in the rest of the area with glue. When you are on your last row closest to the area's wall or end, use a random plank to get the measurement. Put the plank you want to put in the last row on top of the row right before it and line up the edges. Use your random plank to measure the size you need by putting it on top and pushing the tongue side all the way against the wall. Use a pencil to mark the plank you want to cut along the groove side of the random plank you are using for measuring. Cut the plank using a table saw. Using another plank to get your measurement, you will get the cutting line you need and the ¼ inch expansion gap you need around the floor's edges. Put the plank in the glue and use a pry bar to fit it tightly to the row before it. If a plank will not go in easily, use a pull bar and hammer. You can also use a hammer and tapping block or pull bar if the butt joints do not close easily. Once you have your last row in, make sure it is pushed down all the way into the glue by using your pry bar against the wall and pushing down on the floor. Tape the last rows to the rows before them, and then you can start on the other side of the room or area you are working in. Start by snapping another chalk line and filling in the area as you did on the other side of the initial straight line.

Repeat the entire process until the whole area is filled in completely. Once complete, move to Chapter 6, "Trim."

Installed as a Floating Floor

Engineered hardwood installed as a floating floor can be installed in one of two ways depending on preference. You can start by making a straight-line in the middle of the room as you would with a glue down, or you can start from a wall or existing floor. If the area you are working in is exceptionally large, it is probably better to start in the center of the room with a straight-line for aesthetic reasons. Starting from a straight-line will help to reduce your last row from being narrow on one end and wider on the other. If a wall is really off, this will end up happening anyways. If the area you are working in is narrow, or you don't mind if your last row is not uniform all the way down, you can start off of a wall or existing floor edge. Starting from a wall or existing floor is the typical method for the installation of floating floors. Starting from a straight-line is sometimes difficult because the floating floor tends to shift as you install them. The tools needed to install either method will be a pencil, hammer, tapping block, pry bar, pull bar, a miter saw, and table saw. If you must make rounded cuts, a jigsaw will also be required.

Straight-Line Method

If you are going to start from a straight-line, you will need a tape measure, chalk line, nail that can be driven into the subfloor, a hammer, and possibly spacers depending on the area you are working in. Measure the room or area you are working in perpendicular to the direction of how the floor is going. Measure both ends of the room or area you are working in and find what would be closest to the center. Once you find your center make two marks as you would before. The subfloor will be covered with some underlayment, so you may not be able to make a mark with a pencil depending on the type of underlayment and may have to use a marker. Once you have your marks in the desired spots, hammer a nail into one of them and snap a line described in previous sections. Unlike nailed down or glued down floors, you will not need to make another line.

Use the chalk line you snapped to align the edge of your planks. Put two planks together end to end and close the butt-joints. Start from one end of the room or area you are working in, making sure to leave a ¼ inch gap between the wall and the first plank.

Some products are tap and lock, and some are drop and lock. The tap and lock product will need to be put together as close as possible and then tapped together using a hammer and tapping block. Put the tapping block on the opposite end of the butt joint of the plank that is not near the wall or edge of the area you are working in. Make sure the tapping block is above the locking mechanism, not pushing against it, so it does not get damaged. Hit your hammer lightly against the tapping block to close the butt joint. If the plank you are tapping on moves the other plank against the wall and does not close the butt joint, put a spacer between the plank and the wall to maintain the ¼ inch gap. If you have a drop and lock product, you just must line the planks up and drop the end of the second plank over the first. Lightly tap the butt joint on the top of the plank with your hammer to close it.

Once you have your first two planks down and lined up with the straight-line, you can put another plank in front of them, making sure it bridges the butt joint that is locked together. Most floating floor products will have to be put in by sliding the next plank in at about a 45° angle and then lightly tapping it with your hammer and tapping block. Once again, make sure your tapping block is above the locking mechanism, not pushing against it. While you are lightly tapping the tapping block, simultaneously push it down toward the subfloor to lock the plank into place. Make sure to read the manufacturer's directions for putting planks together and closing the butt joints. Once you have this plank in, there should be an empty space between it and the wall or edge of the area you are working in. Fill in this gap by turning another plank the opposite way the floor is going and push it against the wall. Mark the spot where the new plank ends; this will be your mark for where to cut. Cut the plank and put it in the spot that needs to be filled. Make sure to leave a ¼ inch gap between the edge of the cut plank and the wall or edge of an existing floor. You will learn how far you should put your cutting mark from the edge of the plank you are using to measure the more you move along with the floor. Keep the other ends of the planks that you cut because they can be used on the floor's opposite ends.

Once you have the second row started, you can start to move down that row and the first row. Start by putting another plank in the second row and tapping it in at about a 45° angle. When the plank is in properly, close the butt joint how described before, whether it is a tap and lock or drop and lock. After you put this next plank in the second row, go back to the first row and put another plank in this row. Continue this process all the way down the length of the room you are working in, making sure that the first row is still lined up with your straight-line. When you get to the edge of the area you are working in, measure your end cuts the way you did for the empty spot in the second row. Turn the planks the opposite way the floor is laying and push the end all the way against the wall or edge of an existing floor. Mark one plank where the edge of the plank ending the first row is, and mark another plank where the plank ending the second row is. Cut your two marked planks and install them at the end of the first and second row. If you have a tap and lock product, you will need to use a pull bar and hammer to close the butt joints. Make sure to leave a ¼ inch gap and keep the other end of the planks you cut for the room's opposite side.

When your first two rows are in place, you can put some weight on and behind them to keep them from moving while you are installing. I like to use the boxes the product comes in. You can now use the other side of the planks you cut for the end of the first two rows. Put these pieces on the other end of the room, the side you started on, and continue the installation process. Make sure to stagger the butt joints keeping them at least the width of the planks apart.

Once you get to the wall or end of the room or area, you will use another plank to get your measurement. Unlike raw wood or tongue and groove engineered hardwood, you will have to take a piece of the locking mechanism off. The locking mechanism will have a raised lip on the edge; cut this piece off using a table saw. Table saws have a guard, sometimes called a fence, that can be adjusted to make sure you cut a straight line. Align the guard to where it will just take off the raised lip from the locking mechanism. This plank with the lip cut off is known as a scribe; it will be used to give you the contour of the wall. The shorter the plank, the better it will be for getting an accurate measurement. I would not cut the plank shorter than 6 to 8 inches because it will take longer than necessary to get an accurate measurement. When you get to the row closest to the wall or edge of the area you are working in, put a plank on the row before it. Line the plank up with both edges of the row and use your scribe by putting it on top of the plank and pushing it up against the wall. Mark the plank by dragging your pencil along the back of the scribe, making sure to move the scribe along the wall until you reach the end of the plank. Continue the process all the way till you reach the end of the row. You will need to use a hammer and pull bar to install the planks near the wall or end of the area. If you are putting in a tap and lock product, you can use either a tapping block or pull bar and a hammer to close the butt joints. When you reach the end of this side of the room or area you are working in, you can put spacers between the wall and the planks. After finishing this side of the room or area you are working in, complete the process on the other side of the straight-line. When you finish installing the entire floor, you can move on to chapter 6 "Trim."

Off of the Wall Method

If you are going to install your product initially starting from a wall, you will need the same tools as before, including flooring spacers. Pick what direction you want your floor to go, and then decide which wall to start from. Outside walls or walls that are around the perimeter of the house are usually the straightest. Another good way to pick which wall or area to start from is which side of the room or area you are working in is the longest. Once you have decided which wall to work from, place a plank in one corner all the way up against the wall. Put a spacer at the end of the plank in between it and the wall. Put two spacers in between the long side of the plank and the wall. Place another plank alongside the wall or edge of the area you are working in and close the butt joint. Put two more spacers in between this plank and the wall. After you have two planks against the wall, put a plank in front of the first two blanks, bridging over the closed butt joint. Use the method described before you turn a plank around to measure the area between the end of the plank in the second row and the end wall from which you started. Use a pull bar and hammer to close the butt joint; if the pull bar does not work, use a pry bar.

Once you have the first two rows started, you can continue down the rows with two more planks. After these planks are in, you can start the third row. Cut a board in between the size of the first plank and the size of the plank at the end of the second row. Make sure to put spacers around all the edges of the planks to keep an expansion gap. Continue to put a new plank in every row, moving down the rows to the end of the room or area you are working in and moving forward in front of the rows you already have down. Make sure to stager the butt joints and keep them at least the width of the planks apart. Continue this process until the entire area is filled in with planks. Remember to keep putting spacers around the edges to maintain your expansion gap and so that while you are installing, the floor does not shift. When you get to the last row nearest to the wall or edge of the area you are working in, use the scribe method as described in the previous section to get the measurements for the last row. Once you have the entire area installed, move on to chapter 6, "Trim."

Floating Floors Other than Engineered Hardwood

You can follow the previous sections' methods for floating floors that are not engineered hardwood, such as laminate and vinyl planks. One difference is that you can use a laminate snapper to get your end cuts instead of a miter saw. Another difference is that laminate and vinyl planks cannot be sanded and refinished, so if the floor gets scratched or gouged, there are not very many options on how to fix it. After you have installed the floor following one of the methods in the previous section, move on to chapter 6, "Trim." If you damage the floor, see chapter 7, "Maintenance," to see if there is something you can do about it.

Glued Down and Peel and Stick Vinyl

Glued down vinyl and peel and stick vinyl are installed much like a glued down engineered hardwood product. You would get your straight line marked out in both instances as described in the section on glued down engineered hardwood. You would spread the adhesive in the marked out area for glue down vinyl and let it flash over or partially dry. Follow the manufacturer's directions for the time it takes to flash over and what kind of trowel to use. Once the adhesive is flashed over, you can start to lay your product in the area. Make sure to stagger the butt joints keeping them at least the product's width apart from each other. For peel and stick products, you would do the same thing, except you do not have to spread any adhesive; peel the paper from the back of the product and stick it down. Many glued down and peel and stick vinyl products are made to look like tile; if this is the case, you do not have to stagger the butt joints. If the product is made to look like tile, you can either line all the tiles up or lay them subway style, meaning the tiles' ends line up with the middle of the tiles next to them. Because glued down vinyl and peel and stick vinyl are usually so thin and don't have a tongue and grove or locking mechanism, the only tools you will need are a utility knife with a sharp blade and possibly a laminate snapper and thin pry bar. Once you have your product completely installed, you can move on to Chapter 6, "Trim."

For the best results on all products, make sure to read the manufacturer's recommendations, and follow them. Follow the manufacturer's instructions exactly to make sure that any manufacturer guarantee will not become void. Once you have installed your product to your liking, you can move on to the next chapter, "Sanding, Staining, and Finishing," If you have a raw wood product, or skip to Chapter 6, "Trim" for all other products.

Chapter 5: Sanding, Staining, and Finishing

Sanding

If you installed a raw hardwood product, you must sand it before applying stain or finish. You can also sand a damaged engineered hardwood product if it has a large enough wear layer. How much sanding you will have to do depends on what you are trying to do with your floor. If you are repairing a scratch in an engineered product, there will be minimal sanding. You may even be able to buff an engineered product if the scratches are not very deep. Look at the section for sanding for natural directions. If you stain a floor a dark color such as graphite or ebony, you will have to do a significant amount of sanding. Whether you are sanding a raw wood product or an engineered product, you will need a drum sander, floor edger, wood scraper, file, and sandpaper for a drum sander and floor edger. For raw wood, you will also need a trowelable wood filler that matches the product you installed. If you are sanding a floor in a kitchen or some other area with cabinets, you may need to use a toe kick edger to get the area under the cabinets.

Each drum sander will have a specific size of sandpaper that corresponds to the drum size. Drum sanders come in 3 standard sizes, 8 inches, 10 inches, and 12 inches. The larger the drum sander, the harder it will be to work with sanding, but you will cover a larger area. Floor edgers come in one size, 7 inches, and toe-kick edgers come in two sizes, 5 inches or 7 inches. Follow the manufacturer's directions for installing the sandpaper onto drum sanders, floor edgers, and toe-kick edgers. You will need 50-grit sandpaper and 100-grit. If you were refinishing a floor that was already finished, you would also need 36 or 40-grit sandpaper. You will also need a buffer pad and a 100 and 220-grit buffer screen.

Sanding for a Natural Coat

Sanding to put on a natural or clear coat is the shortest process next to buff coating a floor with minor scratches. The first step in the sanding process is going around all the floor edges and the areas the drum sander will not reach, a process called edging, with your floor edger. First, use the floor edger with 50-grit sandpaper against the wood's grain, which goes along the length of the planks. Move the edger left and right against the grain, starting from about a foot back from the wall and steadily moving forward about an inch at a time until you get to the edge of the floor. This process is known as cutting. Once you have cut a section of about 2 feet, move the edger up and down along the grain, starting from your left side and moving to the right about an inch at a time. This will smooth out the area you cut; this process is called feathering. Once you have a section cut and feathered, move to you right and do the same thing over about another 2-foot section. You will have to change the sandpaper when it starts to get dull; this will vary depending on the product you are sanding. Softer floors like fir and red oak can be sanded using the same piece of sandpaper over areas of anywhere from about 10 to 20 feet, whereas harder woods such as maple or mahogany can dull a paper in as little as 4 or 5 feet. Continue this edging process until you have the entire perimeter of the floor and any spot where the drum sander cannot fit in, such as small closets, sanded. Make sure to empty the bag catching dust attached to the edger once it starts to get full. If you were refinishing a floor, you would start this whole process with 36-grit sandpaper.

Once you have the area edged with 50-grit sandpaper, you can run the drum sander with 50 grit sandpaper. Make sure the sandpaper is securely attached to the drum sander as it may not sand properly. In some machines, the paper will even tear and explode, which is scary when unexpected. The paper should be fit tightly onto the drum without any loose spots. Once again, make sure to follow the manufacturer's directions completely. When you are sure that the sandpaper is on correctly, you can start the first part of the sanding process, getting the floor flat. When running a drum sander, make what is called a pass by moving the sander forward and then pulling it backward. Drum sanders have a lever that lifts and lowers the drum. Whenever you lift or lower the drum, you must make sure you are in motion, whether you are moving forward or backward. If you come to a stop before lifting or lowering the drum, it will leave what is known as a drum mark. Drum marks are sanded out gouges that take away from the floor being flat.

To make sure the floor is flat, you will have to sand the floor at a 45° angle. If you are sanding an engineered hardwood product to repair it, skip this step. If the scratch is not very deep, move on to the section about buffing. Start from one corner of the room with at least enough room to make a pass, about 4 or 5 feet. Move from the left to the right, starting in one corner and ending up in the opposite corner running at a 45° angle to the floor's direction. Make a pass by slowly dropping your drum as you move forward and then lift it about 8 inches from the wall or edge of the floor while still moving forward. Before hitting the wall, start to move backward and drop your drum while you are moving. While walking backward, move over to where you are about an inch or two from the spot you originally started. Make sure to pick up your drum while still moving before you walk into the wall behind you or hit the edge of the floor. Continue this process, moving over a few inches at a time until you get into the opposite corner of the room. Do this in all corners of the room, always moving from your left to your right.

After you have sanded all areas that you can at a 45° angle, you can straighten them up. To straighten up a room, you must sand with the grain or the planks' length. Always start from the left side of the room or area you are working in and move towards the right side. Make a pass by starting as close to the edge of the floor on your left side and as far back as you can. Remember always to drop and lift your drum while moving. Start moving forward and drop your drum slowly, walking in the direction of the grain. Lift your drum when you get as close as you can to the edge of the floor while still being able to move forward without hitting the wall or something in front of you. Walk slowly backward and drop your drum while in motion. Keep walking backward until you are almost about to run into the wall or edge of the floor and lift your drum while still in motion. Continue this process, moving about an inch or starting from the left and working your way to the right. You should see the sanding marks left from when you were sanding at a 45° angle; you are trying to get rid of these with this process. Once you have sanded from the left side of the room or area you are working in all the way to the right, turn around and do the same thing on the other end of the room. During the sanding process, you will have a bag attached to the sander that collects dust from the sanding process; make sure to empty the bag when it starts to get full. Depending on the size of the area you are sanding, how hard the wood is, and what size drum sander you are using, you may also have to change your sandpaper.

Once you have sanded all the areas you can with your 50-grit sandpaper on the floor edger and the drum sander, it is time to trowel fill the floor. Make sure you have a product that matches the color of the product you installed. Pour out a puddle that will fill the area you are working in; see manufacturer's recommendations for how much filler you will need. Use a flat trowel with no teeth to spread the filler around the floor, making sure to get it into all the cracks. Do not spread the filler on too thick, or it will take a long time to dry and will gum up your sandpaper, making it almost useless. Spread the filler across the whole floor and allow it to dry if the manufacturer recommends. Some deep cracks or gouges may take longer to dry than the rest of the floor.

Once the filler is dry, you can run the 100-grit, your final sandpaper. Start by edging the same way as described in the section before, but this time you will be trying to get the wood fill off while sanding with the 100-grit sandpaper. Do not worry about any filler in the corners or hard to reach areas because you will get that later by hand. After you have edged the entire perimeter and the areas the drum sander can 't reach, run the 100-grit on the drum sander. This time you do not have to run the drum sander at a 45°angle because the floor is already flat. Just run the sander with the grain starting from the room's left side, working toward the right side. Make sure to run the sander slow enough to get the filler off the floor. After reaching the right side of the room, turn around and do the other side of the room, working from left to right.

After you have done all your edging and drum sanding, you can get all the corners and hard to reach areas with a wood scraper and a piece of 50-grit sandpaper. Scrape with the direction of the grain, all the corners, and areas you could not reach with the sanders. After scraping the hard to reach areas, sand them with the grain by hand using a piece of 50-grit sandpaper. I typically use a piece of edger paper folded in half. After you do all your handwork, you have to buff the floor. Use a buffer pad and a 100-grit buffer screen on your buffer. Buff around the perimeter of the floor and then work your way across the entire floor, moving along the floor's direction. Once you have buffed the entire floor, it will be ready for a natural coat called a clear coat.

Sanding for a Stained Floor

If you stain a floor, you will follow the same process described in the previous section, except the buffing stage will come a little later. Follow all the steps before, but after you do your handwork in the hard to reach areas, you will have to keep hand sanding the floor's edges. The floor edger leaves little swirl marks around the areas you edged. When you stain a floor, especially when you stain it a dark color, the marks left from edging become noticeable. To remove these marks, you will have to sand them out with 50-grit sandpaper. Sand all the areas you edged with the direction of the grain. There will be an area where the marks from the edger stop and the drum sander begin; make sure to sand past this point to where the sanding looks consistent. In areas where the drum sander could not reach, such as small closets, you will have to hand sand the entire area. After you hand sand all the marks left from the edger, you can buff the floor as described before and move on to the staining process.

Staining

Before staining the floor, your desired color, vacuum the floor well. Make sure to read all the manufacturer's directions to know what conditions work best for the stain, such as room temperature and humidity. The stain is typically applied using a towel or some cloth rag. Some professionals use an applicator attached to a long stick, but this is unnecessary, considering you will have to wipe the stain off using a towel or cloth rag. You will need several clean, dry rags to wipe excess stain off as well as a bucket for the stain and a bucket or bag to throw used rags into. Pour all the stain you will need for the desired area into one bucket and mix well. On the directions, it will tell you how much area the stain should cover. Remember, it is always better to be over than under, so round up when you are calculating how many cans of stain to use. The same thing goes for how many dry rags you use; the more, the merrier. There is no real way to know how many rags you will need to use because they have different sizes, textures, and absorbencies, depending on the material. A good rule of thumb is a standard 12-inch by 12-inch terry cloth towel will wipe off about 20 to 25 square feet of stain.

Once you have all your stains, rags, and buckets together, you can start the staining process. Make sure to wear some gloves, either latex, vinyl, or nitrile, while staining. Put one rag into the bucket of stain and soak it completely. Wipe the rag on the floor in the direction that the grain is going. Wipe from one end of the room towards the other, covering a 2 to 3-foot section as you move. On the stain's directions, there will be a certain amount of time stated that you should wait for the stain to set in. Once you have waited the stated amount of time, wipe all the excess stain off using two dry rags, one in each hand. Make sure to wipe all the excess off and then wipe in the grain's direction once you have wiped all the start from one side of the room and apply stain moving towards the other side. Cover a 2 to 3-foot section making sure to overlap the area you already stained. Wipe this section off as described before and repeat the process until the whole floor is stained. It is best not to walk on the floor right after it is stained, so try to plan how you will stain the floor and get out of the area without walking on it. If you must walk on the floor, you can use two rags, one on each foot, to shuffle your way off the floor. Once the entire floor has been stained, you will have to wait the recommended dry time before you put the finish on.

Finishing

The finish is a chemical compound used to seal a floor and give it the desired sheen. There are several different kinds of finishes, but they come in two basic categories, oil-based and water-based. Both types of finish have their benefits and drawbacks. The oil-based finish has a longer dry time meaning it is somewhat easier to work with, but you must wait longer before applying your next coat. The water-based finish dries fast, but this means that it is difficult to work with. The oil-based finish is a lot less expensive than water-based, but it has a strong odor. The water-based finish is eco-friendly, but it cost more. Whether or not you choose an oil-based or water-based finish, they will come in different sheens. There are four basic sheens to finish ranging from least shiny to most: matte, satin, semi-gloss, and hi-gloss. You will have to consider all the above factors to decide which product works best for your situation. Make sure to vacuum the floor before applying any finish.

Oil-based Finish

When applying an oil-based finish, you will need a bucket, a wood floor finish applicator, and a paintbrush. Make sure to read the manufacturer's recommendations for the exact kind of applicator and brush. Read the instructions for the amount of finish you will need to use for the desired area. Pour all the finish into one bucket and mix well. Start by using the paintbrush to get the entire sidewall, the walls parallel to the floor, the area you are in, and about 5 or 6 feet off the end walls, the walls perpendicular to the floor. Brush the finish in the grain's directions, starting from right next to the wall to about 6 inches away from the wall. Lift the brush up off the floor as you move away from the wall; this is known as feathering, which should not be confused with the feathering described in the edging process. Pour a small puddle on one end of the room and use the floor finish applicator to spread the finish on the area between the end walls you feathered. Make sure to go with the direction of the floor as you apply the finish with the applicator. Once you have filled the area, you have feathered, feather another 5 or 6 feet along the end walls, and repeat the process.

Make sure you have a plan of how you will apply finish to the entire floor and still be able to get off it. Unlike the staining process, you will not be able to walk on the floor right after it is finished. Since you are using an oil-based product, you have a lot of time to work with before the finish dries. A long dry time means you can apply finish to one side of an area and move to the other and then meet in the middle. Once you have applied finish on the entire floor, your first coat is done. The oil-based finish will require three coats. Make sure to clean your applicator and brush with mineral spirits or paint thinner between each coat.

After your first coat has dried, typically about 12 hours, you can start your second coat. Before you start to apply finish again, you will have to buff the floor again. This time instead of a 100-grit screen, buff the floor with a 220-grit screen. After buffing the floor, make sure to vacuum it well. Once the floor is vacuumed, go ahead and apply another coat of finish just as you did before. Let the second coat dry and check how it feels before your final coat. If the floor is ruff to the touch, go ahead and buff the floor with the 220-grit screen again before vacuuming and coating. If the floor is smooth to the touch, skip the buffing process and vacuum and coat it.

Water-based Finish

If you use a water-based finish, you will need a floor finish applicator and a foam applicator pad for the floor's edges. Once again, make sure to read the manufacturer's directions for the exact type of applicator and foam pad. Depending on the type of water-based finish you use, you may use two products, sealer and finish. Just like it sounds, the sealer seals the floor, and the finish is used to give the floor its sheen. With a water-based finish, you will not need a bucket because you will work out of the container it comes in. Some water-based finishes also come with hardeners, which I would not recommend if you want to reuse your finish for another application.

The process for using the sealer and the finish are the same, except you apply the sealer first. Start by shaking the container of sealer very well and then placing a screen into the pour spout. There should be a screen included with the product. Pour a line about 1 inch thick of sealer about 4 or 5 inches from the sidewall. Pour the line all the way from one end of the room to the other. Use the foam applicator pad to wipe the line around the edge of the floor, going with the floor's direction. Make sure to apply the sealer to the entire edge of the floor the width of the applicator pad. Make sure there are no dry spots. Pour a small puddle at one end of the room and apply the sealer to the floor at the end, and spread it across a 2-foot section the width of the foam applicator. Spread the sealer making sure to get the entire edge with no dry spots. Feather the 2-foot section by pulling the foam pad starting from the wall away from the wall about 8 inches, lift off the floor as you do so. Do the same thing on the other end of the room, and then pour a line of sealer along the length of the sidewall about 2 inches thick. Pour the line bout the width of the applicator pad away from the sidewall and starting and stopping the same distance from the end walls. Fill in the entire area between areas you feathered using the floor finish applicator. Repeat this process over the entire area of the floor, making sure there are no dry spots.

Like with stain and oil-based finish, it is best to plan how you will coat the whole floor and be able to get off it. Unlike stain, you cannot walk on the finish after it is applied, and unlike oil-based finish, water-based finish dries fast. Because the water-based finish dries fast, you cannot leave it on one side of the floor and work on the other side with a good amount of time to work in between. If you have to work on one side of the floor and then the other to meet in the middle, you will have to run back and forth to keep each side wet enough to work with continually. And when I say "run' sometimes I mean you actually have to run. To keep a section wet enough to work with, you will have to apply a sealer or finish over about a 6-inch section instead of a 2-foot section and then go back and work on the other section. You will only work in each section for a few minutes before the other starts to dry. If the sections are large or far apart, you will have to run from section to section, so make sure to plan out how you will coat the floor before you start.

Once your first coat of sealer is dry, which can be as little as an hour or two, it will be ready to buff. Buff water-based finish and sealer with a buffer pad and 220-grit sandpaper. Buff the floor and vacuum before applying another coat of sealer as described before. For water-based finishes, the floor will get 2 coats of sealer and 2 coats of finish. Once the second coat of sealer is dry, which will take about 2 or 3 hours, buff the floor just as before and then vacuum. Apply the finish just like you did the sealer. The first coat of finish will take a little longer than the sealer to dry because the floor is sealed and no longer porous. After the first coat of finish is dry, check if it is ruff to the touch. If the floor is still ruff, go ahead and buff it again, but if it is smooth, vacuum it and apply the final coat of finish. The final coat should take the longest to dry but still should not take longer than 4 hours. Once the floor is finished, you can put trim around all the exposed edges.

Chapter 6: Trim

Trim

Even after your floor has been installed, and if necessary, sanded and finished, there is still one more step before your floor is complete. There will be gaps around all the floor edges that will need to be covered with a trim piece. The type of trim piece you will need depends on what is on the other side of the gap. If there is a wall on the other end of the gap, people typically use a baseboard. Sometimes people will use quarter round or base shoe instead of the baseboard or in combination with baseboard depending on preference. Quarter round and base shoe are most often used around cabinets if the toe-kick underneath does not cover the gaps. If there is another floor on the other side of the gap, an end cap, t-molding, or reducer will need to be used depending on the type of floor and how much different in height they are. In some cases, there are several different trim options, and it depends on your personal preference.

Baseboard

Baseboard is the most common type of trim used to cover gaps that are next to walls. Sometimes baseboard is used to trim around cabinets, fireplaces, and other areas where it will fit. There are several different sizes, styles, and types of baseboards. The most common type of baseboard is made up of MDF or medium-density fiberboard, but there are also wood and plastic options. MDF baseboard will need to be painted; I recommend painting it before installation. The wood baseboard can be painted or stained to match the floor. Plastic baseboard is usually used in wet areas such as bathrooms or kitchens and comes in a variety of colors, including grain patterns that match laminate and vinyl floors. Make sure to order enough baseboard to cover the entire length of the area you are going to install it in and add 10% to account for cutting waste. You will need a tape measure, pencil, miter saw, air compressor, air hose, and an 18-gauge brad nailer to install the baseboard.

When installing the baseboard, you will want to start from a door jam, cabinet, or some other area where the baseboard will end. Use your tape measure to get the length of the area you are going to put the baseboard in. Every time whatever you are putting the baseboard on changes directions or comes to an end, this will be a different piece of baseboard. If you are putting the baseboard in a corner or wrapping around a corner, you will need to cut the two pieces of baseboard going in or around that corner at half the angle of the corner. This means that if you are putting the baseboard in or around a 90°angle, you will cut the two pieces of baseboard that end on this corner at 45° angles. In most homes, most angles will either be 90° or 45°. If there are angles that look to be different, you may need an angle finder to get a proper cut. If you are cutting the baseboard to fit into a corner, the angle will be cut to where the front of the baseboard is shorter than the back. If you are cutting the baseboard to fit around a corner, the angle will be cut to where the front of the baseboard is longer than the back. Once you have the baseboard cut to length, you can nail it in with your brad nailer. Shoot one nail every 12 to 16 inches if the baseboard is shorter than 4 inches. If the baseboard is 4 inches or taller, shoot two nails, one about two inches above the other, every 12 to 16 inches. For the best results, shoot your nails into the studs of the wall; this may require the use of a stud finder.

Once you have all the baseboard installed, you will want to put on the finishing touches. If you used a painted baseboard, you would want to caulk the top of the baseboard with caulking that matches the baseboard's color or the wall. If you used a wood baseboard that matches the floor's color, this is typically not necessary. You will also want to use a matching painter's putty to fill in the nail holes. If you used a painted baseboard, you might have to go back and do some touch-up painting on the nail holes and other trouble areas.

Base Shoe and Quarter Round

Base shoe and quarter round are often used along with baseboard but can be used instead as well. They are most typically used underneath cabinets to cover gaps between the floor and toe-kicks. Base shoe and quarter round usually come in colors or grain patterns that match the floor, but they can also come in wood or MDF that can be painted. They are installed just as you would install the baseboard, except you do not have to nail them into a stud because they are so short. They can also be glued into areas where a bard nailer will not reach. If you are installing base shoe or quarter round with baseboard, install the baseboard first. Like baseboard, you will have to putty the nail holes but typically do not have to caulk the top or do touch-ups unless you painted the base shoe or quarter round.

__End Caps, T-moldings, Reducers, and Other Transitions__

If there is another floor on the other side of the gap, a piece of baseboard, base shoe, or quarter round typically will not be right for the job. If there is carpet on the other side of the floor, you can use an end cap or metal transition strip. End caps come in colors that match the floor and are the typical choice for installers. Metal transition strips are typically used when carpet meets tile, but I have seen them used with raw wood meeting carpet, typically in older homes. If your floor is meeting with another hard surface floor, which is anything other than carpet, and the floor is about the same height as the floor you installed, you would install a t-molding. If the floor is another hard surface and it is either higher or lower than the one you installed, you will need a reducer.

Whichever type of transition you are installing, they can be installed with either a strong construction adhesive or nails. If you are using transitions that come with a laminate or vinyl product, they will typically have some locking system attached to the subfloor. The transition strip will then be attached to the locking system. If your floor is on a wood subfloor, the locking system will be nailed or screwed in place. If the subfloor is concrete, the locking system will most likely be glued in place. Follow the manufacturer's directions for the best results. Sometimes, I glue transitions instead of using the locking mechanism because they are not always the most secure. If your floor is on a concrete subfloor and your product does not come with a locking system for transitions, glue the transition in place and tape it with masking tape to secure it while it dries. If your floor is on a wood subfloor, it is not raw wood or engineered hardwood, and it does not come with a locking system for transitions, go ahead and glue the transitions in with a construction adhesive and tape them while they dry. If you have a raw wood or engineered hardwood product on a wood subfloor, go ahead and nail the transitions in place. If you have a raw wood transition, it will have to be hand sanded with 50-grit sandpaper and stained to match if necessary and then finished. Raw wood transitions can be installed after the finishing process of the floor or right before. If you have a transition that was nailed in, you will have to fill in the nail holes with a matching painter's putty or wood filler.

If there are any small gaps that a piece of trim will not cover or would not look appropriate to cover, you can fill these in with caulk. Makes sure that the caulk matches the floor or whatever the gap is next to, such as the wall, baseboard, metal, or another floor. Some gaps will look better if you feel them in with caulk instead of a transition. This is usually the case around door thresholds and slider door frames. Find a caulk that matches either the threshold, door frame, or floor and use a piece of tape to tape off the area. Tape along the floor and along the threshold or door frame. Squirt the caulk into the gap using a caulking gun and press along the entire area with your finger removing excess caulk. Make sure there are no gaps in the caulk; it should look even. When the caulk looks consistent, pull the tape, and you should be left with a nice straight line of caulk.

Once you have all the transitions in place and every gap in the floor covered, your floor is complete. There may be some dust and debris leftover from the installation of the trim. Make sure to give the floor one more good vacuuming. There still might be some dust or scuff marks left on the floor after vacuuming. The next chapter on maintenance will discuss how to remove that and keep the floor looking as new as possible.

Chapter 7: Maintenance

Maintenance

Now that you have a nice new floor, you will want to keep it looking that way. When you have completed your floor and all the necessary trim, there still might be some dust or scuff marks left on the floor. You should be able to just dry mop or dust mop your floor, and it will take care of the dust left behind. For scuff marks, you will want to use a cleaner that is compatible with your floor. Depending on the product you ended up installing, there are several different options for cleaners to choose from.

Raw Wood

Raw hardwood should not be wet mopped often because of a few different factors. If you ended up using an oil-based finish, the only concern with wet mopping is that with excessive use, the floor may start to swell if water somehow gets into it. If you used a water-based finish, the water might start to deteriorate the finish over time. There are floor cleaners made specifically for wood floors that would be your best option. Some brands are made by the same company as some finishes that would work best with their finish if you happened to use such a finish. For the best results, make sure to follow the floor cleaner manufacturer's directions for use. I would not recommend using floor cleaners very often as they can leave a visible film on top of the finish over time. For the most part, dry mopping or dust mopping with a microfiber mop should be fine.

If you have furniture on top of the floor, make sure to use felt glides underneath where the furniture and floor make contact. This will help with any possible scratching if the furniture moves. If you use area rugs on the floor, make sure to move them a few inches every couple of weeks, especially if there is a significant amount of sunlight entering the room. Move the rugs in different directions every time you do; this will help to avoid a shadow developing underneath the rug where light does not hit the floor.

If the floor receives heavy foot traffic, you may start to see tiny scratches on the surface of the finish. If the scratches are not very deep, you can buff the floor and refinish it. This is called a buff coat. You buff the floor with a 100-grit screen, then vacuum it and coat it. After the finish dries, you buff the floor again with a 220-grit screen and then vacuum and coat it one more time. Buff coating a floor is a much cheaper alternative to sanding the floor again and refinishing it. I would recommend doing this every 3 or 4 years for a floor that receives a lot of foot traffic or in homes with pets such as cats or dogs.

Engineered Hardwood

Engineered hardwood, just like raw wood, should not be wet mopped very often. There are products made specifically for wood floors that would be a better alternative to a wet mop. Once again, I would not recommend using cleaners very often as they can leave a film on top of the finish of the floor.

Just like a raw wood floor, you also want to use felt glide underneath any furniture in direct contact with the floor. Also, stagger area rugs as described in the previous section.

Engineered hardwood can be buff coated as described in the previous section if there are scratches on the surface of the finish. Because engineered hardwood comes prefinished before installation, you will have to check with the manufacturer to see what kind of finish they used. You will want to double-check this because if you put a water-finish over a product with an oil-based finish on it or vice-versa, the finishes will not mix, and you will have an ugly looking coat. If the floor you put in was a distressed product, meaning it is not completely flat and may have tiny holes in it, the buffer would not get into the floor's valleys and tiny holes. For distressed floors, it is better to just leave them alone, unless you want to buff them by hand which could take a long time.

Laminate

Laminate floors should not be wet mopped because they will swell if exposed to excessive amounts of water. There are several multipurpose products used for cleaning laminate floors. Some of the products are used for laminate as well as tile, stone, or hardwood. The best products are used specifically for laminate, or laminate and hardwood both. For the best results, make sure to use the manufacturer's directions. Once again, do not use cleaning solutions often as they will leave a film layer on the floor. If you have a scuff mark on the floor, it usually can be taken out with a melamine foam, commonly known as a Mr. Clean® Magic Eraser. If you get a scratch on the floor, you will either have to fill them with a colored putty or replace the scratched planks.

Vinyl

Vinyl is the only wood-like product that can be wet mopped because it is completely waterproof. There are also floor cleaning products used specifically for vinyl and multipurpose products that include vinyl. For the best results, use a product specifically for vinyl and follow the manufacturer's directions. Do not use the floor cleaner often as it will leave a film layer on the floor. Just like with laminate, you can clean scuff marks with a melamine foam or Mr. Clean® Magic Eraser. If you get a scratch on the floor, you will have to either fill it in with colored putty or replace the scratched planks.

Conclusion

For all floors other than vinyl, make sure to clean up any spills right away. Vinyl will not swell because it is waterproof, but all other products will swell to some degree depending on how much of a liquid has spilled and how long it has been on the floor. Laminate flooring will swell more than raw wood and engineered hardwood because it is very porous underneath the top layer. Raw wood is the only product that you can sand down a significant amount, making it one of the most repairable products. All products can be repaired or replaced; it just takes the right materials and the right know-how.

The best way to ensure that your floor will last as long as it should and ensure any product guarantees is to follow all the manufacturer's directions and recommendations. Sometimes products will be on clearance because they are being discontinued; this sounds like a great deal, but you will not get more product once it is sold out. This is not a problem if you will completely replace the floor down the road, but if you plan on having it for a long time, you may have to replace some parts of it.

Now that you have your brand-new floor installed, it is time to live on it and enjoy it. I hope this book has helped you with all your hardwood flooring needs.

About the Expert

Marc Hagan has been involved in the hardwood flooring industry in California for over 20 years. His father has been sanding, staining, refinishing hardwood floors, and installing new ones since Marc was six years old. Marc and his two older brothers would go with their father and observe the hardwood flooring process. One of his older brothers started his own hardwood flooring business after five years of working in the industry. Shortly after, Marc came along to help his brother with his business. Marc has been working with his older brother at his hardwood flooring business for over five years now.

HowExpert publishes quick 'how to' guides on all topics from A to Z by everyday experts. Visit HowExpert.com to learn more.

Recommended Resources

- HowExpert.com – Quick 'How To' Guides on All Topics from A to Z by Everyday Experts.
- HowExpert.com/free – Free HowExpert Email Newsletter.
- HowExpert.com/books – HowExpert Books
- HowExpert.com/courses – HowExpert Courses
- HowExpert.com/clothing – HowExpert Clothing
- HowExpert.com/membership – HowExpert Membership Site
- HowExpert.com/affiliates – HowExpert Affiliate Program
- HowExpert.com/writers – Write About Your #1 Passion/Knowledge/Expertise & Become a HowExpert Author.
- HowExpert.com/resources – Additional HowExpert Recommended Resources
- YouTube.com/HowExpert – Subscribe to HowExpert YouTube.
- Instagram.com/HowExpert – Follow HowExpert on Instagram.
- Facebook.com/HowExpert – Follow HowExpert on Facebook.